Parts Work

An Illustrated Guide to
Your Inner Life

by **Tom Holmes,** Ph.D
with **Lauri Holmes,** MSW

illustrations by **Sharon Eckstein,** MFA
book design by **Jane Eckstein,** BA

ISBN: 978-0-9798897-1-4
SAN: 854-6614

Winged Heart Press
Highpointe Dr.
Kalamazoo, MI 49008
partswork@wingedheart.org

Thomas R. Holmes
Parts Work: An Illustrated Guide to Your Inner Life

We gratefully acknowledge the following for permission to reprint material. Coleman
Barks, translator, *We are Three: New Rumi Poems* (1987). Athens, Georgia: Maypop Books;
The Illuminated Rumi (1997). New York: Broadway Books. Used by permission of the
author.

Library of Congress Cataloging in Publication Data
Thomas R. Holmes
Parts Work: An Illustrated Guide to Your Inner Life
Includes bibliographical references

Fourth Edition

1. Psychotherapy. 2. Personality. 3. Self awareness
4. Psychology spirituality 5. Subpersonalities

Acknowledgments

This book is the result of the efforts of many people. The foremost is my wife and dearest life companion, Lauri. Not only did she connect me with Richard C. Schwartz in the first place, but she has watched and nourished this book during its long incubation over the past five years. During the past four months, when a midwife was needed to make the birth possible, she has stepped in as editor, encourager, supporter in countless ways and at times as co-author. Our use of the "parts work" process with each other as we have gone through the final stages of putting this book together allowed us to navigate the turbulent waters of this kind of creative partnership in a way that has deepened the love and understanding in our relationship. In chapter seven, which we co-authored, you can see an example of how we used this "parts work" in our relationship.

The other central person in this book is, of course, Sharon Eckstein, who illustrated it with such creativity, skill and insight. Her unusual ability to represent the universal in the personal is what gave me the inspiration to present an illustrated guide to the internal system. The enthusiastic response of those seeing her drawings gave me the momentum to bring it into reality.

I am very grateful to Richard Schwartz for giving birth to the IFS model and nourishing it over the years. I have fond memories of the years in his training groups in the late 1980s which helped give me a new vision of therapy that continues to grow and develop to this day.

I also want to thank those people who were central to my development as a psychotherapist. Mal Robertson, the primary professor in my clinical psychology program, offered both an effective model for training therapists and a chance for me to discover my own love of teaching others. Gene Ballard has been my clinical supervisor, lifelong mentor and model of the embodiment of therapeutic presence and ongoing intellectual inquiry.

As my psychotherapy teachers have been important, so have my spiritual teachers. Pir Vilayat Inyat Khan initiated me into the Sufi Universalist path of the heart, Atum O'Kane has been a wise and loving mentor on that path and Taj Inayat helped me deepen my connection to the path of the heart in recent years. Vietnamese Buddhist teacher Thich Nhat Hanh and the monks and nuns of his order offered me the concepts of Buddhist psychology central to this book and also served as the living embodiment of mindfulness and compassion in everyday life.

The Holistic Health Program at Western Michigan University provided a place in academia where I could explore and teach the integration of spirituality and psychotherapy. I would like to thank the faculty, staff, graduate assistants and students who have given me support over the years. I also want to acknowledge Peter Findeisen, Karin Puescher-Findeisen and the staff of the Caduceus Klinik in Germany for inviting me to offer my teachings on the integration of spirituality and psychotherapy and providing an important opportunity to stay connected to the Sufi path.

Another important source of support has been the training groups over the past three years in which Sharon Eckstein, Judy Whitehurst, Karina Mirsky and Inta Dzelma have participated. Their ability to look deeply into the nature of the internal system and how it heals has contributed to my appreciation of the wonderful healing capacities of this work.

I have gratitude and respect for all those who have entered into the healing journey with me individually or in workshops. I believe that their courage and determination to bring healing and balance to their own personal lives, to face pain and fear while awakening love and understanding, not only heal themselves but help heal the world as well.

I especially want to thank Jane Eckstein for her time, creativity and skill in bringing Sharon's illustrations and the text together in the form of this book. I also want to thank Kathy Jennings for her editorial consultation at a critical time in the process and Paula Jamison for her thoughtful and thorough help in editing the copy.

I also want to express our gratitude to Bob and Louise Dunbar and to Bill and Betsy Maxon for generously making available refuge that allowed this book to be written.

Last but not least, I want to acknowledge my father and mother, Durwood and Mary Holmes. I carry their loving understanding and presence with me in all that I do.

Table of Contents

Introduction

In the early 1980s, Richard C. Schwartz developed a new approach to individual therapy known as the Internal Family Systems (IFS) model. His model provided a systemic approach to working with what many psychologists have called subpersonalities or ego states. John Rowan summarized the work of these psychologists in his book *Subpersonalities* (1990).

This book represents my own variant of the IFS model as I have used it for nearly twenty years in clinical practice, in the classroom with graduate students at Western Michigan University, and in workshops and trainings throughout the United States and Europe. Based on these years of clinical and teaching experience, I am attempting to share my understanding of why we think, feel and act as we do and how we can move toward harmony and balance in our inner and outer lives

The illustrations by Sharon Eckstein used in this book had only been shown as a power point presentation until this book was published. In my workshops and trainings in the United States and Europe I had been urged again and again to publish this illustrated guide to the internal system using Sharon's drawings. These drawings have delighted people around the world and have helped to make this internal systems model more accessible. With this book my hope is to combine these illustrations with an everyday language text which will be useful to therapists, patients and the general public in understanding this unique and effective way of understanding human behavior. For those interested in the IFS model in more detail and in its original form, I recommend reading the book written by Richard C. Schwartz, Introduction to the Internal Family Systems Model (2001)

I have chosen the phrase "Parts Work" as the title for this book. "Parts Work" is the informal way that IFS therapy is referred to by most IFS therapists and clients. The term "parts" refers to the experience of having shifting states of mind that have unique sets of thoughts, feelings and behaviors. When these states of mind reflect patterns of thoughts and feelings that recur often we refer to them as different parts of our selves. Our references to "parts" as separate entities, then, is a sort of shorthand for these repeating patterns of thoughts, feelings and behavior which we experience. This process is explained in detail in Chapter 1.

It is a stretch for some readers to imagine that a part of us can have a wish or intention "of its own." But at times it does seem that in one state of mind we have one set of feelings or desires while in another state we have very different ones. By thinking of these states as separate units, we are able to gain a perspective on ourselves that is quite useful, and by engaging in the state of mind we call "Self" we can be in charge of using the energy of these different mind sets to orchestrate a more balanced life. This is the goal of parts work.

So, although at times during this book we seem to be thinking of parts as almost separate personalities who somehow reside in our minds, characters who have feelings, fight with each other, and dominate our thinking, we are not suggesting that all of us suffer from what is known as Multiple Personality Disorder. MPD is characterized by the defense known as "splitting," where the memories of severe trauma experienced in childhood are completely split off from consciousness. The result of this splitting is that the person seems to be an entirely different personality at different times. These personalities often have no knowledge of each other. This is the opposite of the goal of parts work, which is to increase our understanding of all of our parts.

There is another centered place of consciousness where we can witness or observe these "parts" or patterns of thoughts and feeling we are experiencing. We refer to this state of mind as the "Self." By developing the "Self" we can bring harmony and balance to our psychological system. This is the primary goal of Internal Family Systems Therapy.

The "Parts Work" model presented here combines the IFS model with several central concepts about the nature of consciousness found in Buddhist psychology as presented in the teachings of Buddhist teacher and scholar Thich Nhat Hanh (2001, 2006). I find it exciting that a late twentieth-century systemic model of the psyche and ancient Buddhist teachings on the nature of consciousness fit so well together. In addition to using these Buddhist concepts as part of the basic formulation of this book, I give several chapters to integrating the spiritual life of the client into psychotherapy using the parts work model. The IFS model of therapy combined with spiritual understanding and practice offers the most effective model of psychotherapy I have found in my thirty-five years of studying, practicing and teaching. This way of working integrates easily with the spiritual life of the client, and when such integration occurs it becomes even more effective. I discuss and illustrate the integration of spirituality into the therapeutic process in Chapter 8.

As a teacher, I have been interested in finding a way to share the insights offered by this therapy model with a wider audience. This book is designed for that audience. It is about getting to know ourselves in all our inner dimensions. In order to give the reader a complete picture of how the inner system operates we have included in the later chapters detailed accounts of long term therapy. It is through understanding the inner system that we can learn to accept and integrate all the different parts of ourselves and thus develop the capacity to transform those inner patterns of thought, feelings and behavior that cause ourselves and others to suffer. It is with this intention that Lauri, Sharon and I have developed this book. We hope you will find it an interesting and enjoyable way to understand yourself and others.

Tom Holmes

Kalamazoo, Michigan, September, 2010

Chapter 1

Introduction to Parts Work

"There's a part of me . . ."

We are often surprised at how differently we react to various situations. It is almost as if we are a different person at different times. There are many common expressions that describe this experience: "I was beside myself;" he just "pushes my buttons" "I wasn't myself." Or we'll say about someone, "When he gets into a classroom he really goes into his head" or, "She's really shy, but when she gets on stage, wow!" or, "When he's in a negotiation meeting he turns into a Pit Bull."

We also can react to the same situation in different ways, depending on recent events that have occurred in our mental or physical state. In the Buddhist tradition these states are called mental formations or habit patterns. Piaget and the cognitive behaviorist refer to them as schemas. Psychosynthesis refers to them as subpersonalities and psychodynamic psychologists refer to them as ego states. We will call them "parts."

"Picturing" the Inner World

The next illustration represents a Buddhist perspective on the nature of consciousness as presented by Thich Nhat Hanh. This Buddhist model integrates easily with the internal systems perspective of parts work. He uses a circle to represent two important levels of consciousness.

The bottom half of the circle represents the "store consciousness". In it are stored the seeds that contain all of the potential states of mind that we human beings might have. Some of these states of mind seem to occur over and over again in our lives. These regularly occurring states of mind are what we are calling our parts.

The top half of the circle represents our everyday consciousness, what Thich Nhat Hanh calls the "living room" of our consciousness. When the state of mind or part of us comes into the foreground, taking over our thoughts, feelings and behaviors, we say it is in the living room. Buddhist psychology points out that when internal and external conditions support it, a particular state of mind will arise; when those conditions no longer support it, it will go back down into store consciousness.

As long as certain parts are not active in our everyday consciousness, they reside in the store consciousness.

In the store consciousness are seeds of all of our parts and potential parts which have yet to emerge. Some parts are temporarily in "storage," waiting for the right time and situation to come up into the living room of our mind. The seeds carry habit energies from our genetic, cultural and personal history. Carl Jung would see them as having an archetypal basis in past collective experiences. There are hundreds of seeds that could develop if the conditions were right. However, most of us have a primary cast of characters, which could number a dozen or more, a handful of which are the main players in our system.

Is your interested part activated now as you read this book?

A good way to understand how this works is to apply it to your inner system right now. At this moment there might be a variety of parts in your mind that are reacting to this book. It is possible that an interested part of you is activated, a part of you that likes to understand and learn new things.

Perhaps as you are reading now a critical part in you is activated.

If so, a part of you something like this may be in the living room of your mind right now (above).

On the other hand, if you have doubts about what you are reading here, this book may have activated your skeptic or critic part.

It is also possible that both parts are activated at the same time.

It is also possible that these two are able to coexist in your consciousness at this point, and you are interested but cautious.

Depending upon which part of you is in the foreground of your mind, in your "living room," you will experience your world in very different ways. Each of our parts filters our perceptions in their own way. Each has a particular way of seeing the world, so how you view your life experience varies a lot with which part of you is in the living room.

As we have said, a simple but profound concept from the Buddhist model is that when internal and external conditions are right, a given state of mind, a "part," will rise up into the living room of our mind, into everyday consciousness, and when those conditions change that part will go back down into storage. This is why we can seem to be such different people at different times. The living room of the mind is quite active, with various parts of ourselves that come and go, interacting with each other and the outer world to help us cope with the tasks of everyday life. Some of these parts stay longer than others, and some will not leave the living room when it is time for them to go. These are the thoughts you can't get out of your mind, or feelings you can't shake even when you desperately want them to leave. One of the goals of this book is to bring awareness and intention to the various parts of ourselves so that we may have more harmony and balance in our inner systems.

Example of a Parts Dance

When teaching my classes at the university, I always hope the students can bring their interested student parts to class. I often teach evening classes with graduate students who are parents and also working full time. Sometimes these students are having a hard time getting their interested student parts to class. They are in class, but what I see is their "wiped-out" part, which seems to have taken over the living room of their consciousness. Each part has a job in our system. What I am calling the wiped-out part is signaling overload and exhaustion, and letting the person know that it is time to rest.

Exhausted parts let us know that we need rest and relaxation.

However, as is often the case, we do not attend to the messages of one of our parts because other parts are driving us forward. Perhaps caretaker parts were active because someone in the family was sick, thus keeping their worried part and the nurturing part in the living room all night and pushing aside the part that is trying to get us to rest.

In the morning, the multitasker part had to manage other household tasks before leaving for work. By the time evening comes the student is exhausted and her wiped-out part has taken over the living room and is telling her to stop, that it's time to rest. However, her taskmaster" part dragged her body to the classroom anyway. As a result, her physical condition allows her no room for the interested student.

The exhausted part often arises as a result of hard working parts or worry parts taking over for too long.

Remember the principle that when conditions support a part being in the living room of everyday mind it will rise up; when the conditions no longer support it, it will go back down into storage. For the student in my classroom, her manager part is trying to alter her physical conditions by giving her a double espresso coffee. With enough caffeine, and if my lecture is interesting enough to help create the right conditions, the interested student part can return to the living room, with some haranguing from the boss part.

Coffee is one of the ways we intentionally alter the "conditions" in our body to make it more possible for certain parts to arise into our living room. The body is one of the basic elements of the "conditions." We know that when we are tired or sick, grumpy or sad states of mind take over our consciousness much more easily and it is difficult to get our student part into the living room. Psychological, social and other environmental factors are other components making up the conditions that trigger certain parts.

The inner "slave driver" can push us to do things even when we are very tired.

Parts as Psychological Software

The different parts of ourselves are like very sophisticated psychological software designed to get us into the state of mind that will best help us cope with the life tasks facing us. Thus, just as the computer might have an accounting program for keeping track of our finances, we have an analytical part of ourselves that gives us logical information about a situation we might find ourselves in. So we click on the money manager icon in our computer window if we want to balance our budget or pay our bills.

For some people, it is easier to access this money manager program than for others: some may not even know that this program has been loaded onto their computer! For other people, the first reaction to the bills may be a panicked child part; for others, a distracting part may automatically arise so that the task is ignored. Then somehow we find ourselves playing computer games.

While our human software is infinitely more complex and adaptable than the current computer software, this "Windows" analogy can be very useful. The icon on the main menu is a symbol that represents a part of ourselves that can be activated by various situations or people, much like we activate a program by clicking on that icon.

The different parts of ourselves are like psychological software programs designed to cope with specific life situations. These are pictured above as icons on a computer screen.

We have the expression "he really pushes my buttons," which usually refers to a person who activates anger or irritated parts: other people activate different parts of us. Some might activate a romantic feeling; others, fear; others, a playful part of ourselves. The aroma of our favorite food activates our craving part, a little cuddly child might activate our nurturing part, a friendly person might activate our affiliative part, a large barking dog might activate a scared part.

Getting the Right Parts in the Living Room

Having the right parts activated when we need them is not always easy. For example, if we come home from work having been in our business manager parts all day, we may not be able to respond with affection when our sad child, who has been missing us, greets us at the door. Instead, we may ask him if he has done his chores and give him directions about doing his homework before we even greet him properly.

The sad child at the door was hoping that the nurturing part would be available to greet him!

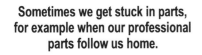

Sometimes we get stuck in parts, for example when our professional parts follow us home.

It can take time to shift into the part that best fits the situation.

The opposite situation can also happen: the parents' nurturing parts are so dominant that they can't discipline the child when it is needed. The ideal is that we have access to the widest range of parts at the time we need them, so that we don't get caught with just a few sets of habitual responses we can make to life's varied situations.

Just as with computer software, getting the program to work properly is not always easy. We might find that when we need to activate a manager program, we can't seem to get away from the games program. Or when we might benefit from having our rational parts manage a situation, our angry or frightened parts take over and get us in trouble.

With computers, we need to know how to get back to the main menu where we can see the icons of all the programs and have access to them. The same is true for the human system. In parts work, the equivalent of the main menu is called the Self. It is the centered place in ourselves where we can access to the appropriate parts when we need them. The next chapter is dedicated to exploring the nature and function of the Self.

The illustrations in this book provide a way for us to understand how parts might show themselves. However, please don't let our images of parts limit how a part might appear for you. All of our systems are unique, so your parts may or may not be like the parts illustrated here. It is also true that parts take on a specific form because they have to play a certain role at times in our lives, and they may take on a totally different shape or form when the conditions change.

Getting a sense of the primary parts in our system is an important step in getting centered. At the end of this chapter, you will find an exercise that offers you a way to identify and explore your primary cast of characters, the parts in your system.

Getting to Know Your Parts

1. Think about some situation in your life that brings on a strong reaction. Here are some ways to clarify the parts that are having this reaction.

- What feelings go with this reaction?

- Where do you feel it in your body?

- What are the thoughts that go with this reaction? What would this part like to say?

- Allow an image to form in your mind that would represent this part. What would it look like?

2. You can also become aware of your primary parts by observing yourself as you go through your daily life. Observe and note:

- What situations activate a part?

- What feelings and actions accompany these parts?

- What function do these parts have?

- How are they trying to help you?

- How do those around you react when you are in that part?

- How do you feel afterwards? Are there other parts that later react to these parts having expressed themselves?

3. If you think of parts as helpers, you might notice that you have several of the following types of parts and you might note them:

- Parts that help you get things done.

- Parts that help you know and assert your needs.

- Parts that help you relax, play and have fun.

Chapter 2

Self in the Inner System

"Can we sit in the center and know?"

"We dance around a ring and suppose, but the Secret sits in the middle and knows."   Robert Frost, 1943

In the center of the inner system there is something that is different in its nature from the parts. This is the place from which we can observe our parts; it is the center of ourselves. In ego psychology it would be called the "observing ego;" Buddhists refer to it as the "witness" or "mindfulness." Richard Schwartz, developer of Internal Family Systems therapy, calls it the "Self." The Self, as we use the term, is the core of our being, the place characterized by mindful awareness, compassionate connectedness and calm, confident clarity.

The Self is the core of our being, from which we can observe our parts with compassion and understanding.

When we are in the Self, we are in a state of awareness quite different from the ordinary but available to anyone. From this place we can see ourselves and others through the kind eyes of non-judgment. We are loving, bemused observers who are very present to our own inner states and to those of the other people we encounter. In this place we let go of anxiety, dissatisfaction, and become aware of our wholeness. Here we can be either passive witnesses or active doers, whichever is called for, and in this state we seem to know clearly what it is we are to do.

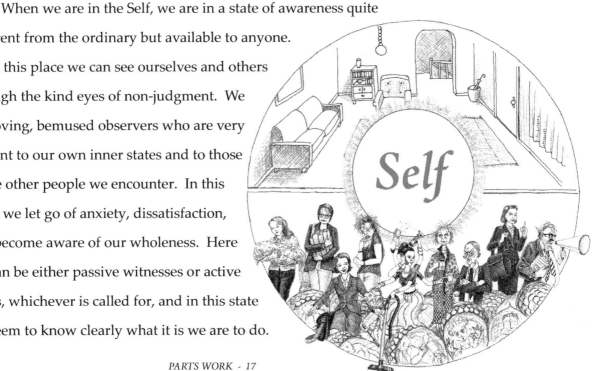

When we are in the state of consciousness we call the Self, we are able to observe the parts but are not taken over by them. For example, there are times when we may become so angry or sad that we are not simply angry or sad, we *are* anger or sadness. In parts work terms, the angry or sad part has blended with us and we are totally in that mind state. It has taken over the whole living room. If we are able to step back from the feeling, then we can get some distance from the engulfing emotion. In that moment the Self can come into the living room of our consciousness.

The Self can be compared to an orchestra conductor who activates appropriate parts when they are needed.

The Self is so subtle that it has been difficult to describe it. One person has said that it is like water: it is clear, and quiet, and calm, and doesn't have a "personality" like the often colorful parts of the inner system do.

Another way of representing Self is to see it as a conductor of an orchestra. All of the parts are the musicians playing the instruments that make the music of our lives. Without the musicians there is no music. Without the conductor the music becomes chaotic, if it begins at all. So when we go to our workplace, the conductor activates the work manager part. When it is time for our nurturing part to be present, the conductor, the Self, quiets the loud brass and may bring out the warm deep stringed instruments of our nurturing parts. So when we are functioning well and in harmony, our conductor, the Self, easily brings forth the parts of ourselves that are needed.

What are the qualities we have when we are in the Self? Richard Schwartz found that when in Self we are calm and compassionate; we have curiosity, clarity, confidence, creativity, courage and connectedness (2003). Roberto Assagioli, the founder of Psychosynthesis, described the Self as the experience of being "able to remain 'centered' in the face of external hardship and internal distress. This experience is of *being*, unshaken by changes in the body, feelings, or mind, always conscious and capable of choice" (in Brown, 1983, 11-12).

Self and Psychological Software

The process of describing Self is perhaps the most challenging task of this book, so I will present a variety of ways for you to try and understand it. To use the computer software model discussed earlier, the Self is like working with the "main menu." The main menu in a computer is one level up in the computer system from the programs themselves. From the main menu we can move to the computer program we need at a given moment. In the same way the Self is on a meta-level of the psychological system, so that from the Self we can move to the part we need for a given situation.

Just as the main menu of a computer is at a level above the software programs, so the Self is at a level above the parts.

However, just as we can sometimes get caught in a computer program and not be able get out, stressful events can result in a part, such as anger, fear or judgment taking over our living room so that we get stuck in that part. We may experience it as a mood we cannot shake. What do you do when you find yourself stuck in a computer program and you can't get out? You shut down and restart. When it starts again you are back in the main menu. This is very much like the human system. We can do a quick reset by giving ourselves time out. Some ways to do this are to go for a walk or have a cup of tea, which brings us back to center, to Self. For stubborn problems we may have to shut the whole system down and go to sleep. When we wake up we are usually back in our Self and can approach the day from a more centered place.

Parents know that when a child gets fussy or grumpy or angry, they may be able to distract the child with something entertaining, or cuddle them into laughing, trying to get the grumpy parts out of the living room. Sometimes, however, the only thing that works is for the child to take a nap. When the child wakes up the system is usually reset and the main menu available.

Self and Poetry

I will continue to offer various ways to help you understand the Self in the hope that several of these descriptions will hit home for you. To go in a very different direction, I have found that poetry offers excellent ways of describing the Self. The quote used at the beginning of the chapter expresses clearly and concisely the experience of Self from a twentieth-century poet. The second quote is from Chuang Tzu, who expressed a similar idea more than 2000 years ago.

> *When we understand, we are at the center of the circle, and there we sit
> while Yes and No chase each other around the circumference.*

> *(in Mitchell, 1993, xv.)*

Our parts dance around our center engaged with the activities of life, making judgments, reacting with yes and no to all kinds of experiences. In our Self we find a place of knowing, a place where we can observe the dance of the different parts of ourselves without either being dominated by or having to cast out various parts of ourselves. These images parallel Carl Jung's description of self as "that center of being which the ego circumambulates" (Singer, 1973).

Perhaps the most direct description of Self comes from Walt Whitman, the nineteenth-century American poet, in his poem, "Song of Myself." Here the difference between our experience of the world from the place of parts is contrasted with the experience of being in Self:

Trippers and askers surround me, people I meet,

The effect upon me of my early life or the ward and city I live in, or the nation,

The latest dates, discoveries, inventions, societies, authors old and new.

My dinner, dress, associates, looks, compliments, dues,

The real or fancied indifference of some man or woman I love,

The sickness of one of my folks or of myself, or ill-doing or loss or lack of money or depressions or exaltations,

Battles, the horrors of fratricidal war, the fever of doubtful news, the fitful events;

These come to me days and nights and go from me again,

But they are not the Me myself.

Apart from the pulling and hauling stands what I am,

Stands amused, complacent, compassionating, idle, unitary,

Looks down, is erect, or bends an arm on an impalpable certain rest,

Looking with side-curved head curious what will come next,

Both in and out of the game and watching and wondering at it.

(Leaves of Grass, 1897)

"Both in and out of the game, watching and wondering at it." This condition of observing while being "in" the game of life yet apart from the "pulling and hauling," is a description of the state of being in Self. The "pulling and hauling," the "fever of doubtful news," offer a fine representation of parts consciousness, the struggle of our state of mind that characterizes our lives when we don't have access to Self. When we are able to access Self we stand "amused, complacent, compassionating, idle and unitary." This phrase depicts the qualities of quiet joy, compassion, an acceptance of things as they are, a deep place of ease and "impalpable certain rest." Whitman could capture so much psychological and spiritual wisdom in these few lines.

Jelaluddin Rumi (1207 -1273) was a famous Sufi poet and mystic revered by those in his religion of Islam as well as by Christians and Jews. He writes:

> *When you do things from your soul,*
> *you feel a river moving in you, a joy.*
> *When actions come from another section, the feeling disappears. . . .*
> *Don't insist on going where you think you want to go.*
> *Ask the way of Spring.*
> *Your living pieces will form a harmony.*
>
> *(trans. Barks, 1987, 44)*

This river of joy is a deep and peaceful feeling of well-being that characterizes the experience of living from the Self. This feeling does not exclude our sadness, anger or fear, but joy arises when we are able to embrace these parts of ourselves and allow them to find their natural balanced place in our lives.

Another poem of Rumi describes the experience of our various parts and how, when one is in the Self, they all are welcome:

> *This being human is a guest house.*
> *Every morning a new arrival.*
> *A joy, a depression, a meanness,*
> *some momentary awareness comes*
> *as an unexpected visitor.*
> *Welcome and entertain them all!*
>
> *(trans. Barks, 1997, 77)*

This passage reflects a core philosophy of parts work: each part has a useful function for the person and we should "treat each guest honorably." When a person is in Self, the parts can be "invited in." The dialog with the parts from Self is the main content of "parts therapy." When the Self can undertake this dialog, the part is able to express its reason for being, the way it is trying to help the person. Through this process the part can begin to lay aside its extreme behavior and assume an effective function in the system.

In the coming chapters we will discuss how parts can become extreme or rigid and how returning to Self helps the parts regain their natural balance and function. To illustrate the change we are talking about, let's take for example an angry part, which might look something like this figure, "Rage." This part is clearly extreme and out of balance and Self is not in the living room. If, however, we were able to create conditions which supported bringing Self into the living room, then this part can transform and take on a more functional form. One client described such a change as can be seen in this illustration. From a rageful, sometimes self-defeating entity it changed over the course of therapeutic dialog into a strong part which can perform the functions of protecting the person without the excessive rage that was a problem for the client and for the client's family and friends.

Another type of part that can provide an example of this shift, is a worried part. Perhaps like the worry of a who is constantly feeling anxious about what might happen. In its extreme form this part could look something like "worry" illustrated here. When Self can be brought into the living room, then this worried part has a chance to shift to a form which allows it to perform its function in an effective way. The useful function of worry is the ability to look ahead and see dangers or risks so the person can be prepared to cope with them. If the person can shift into Self then the worried part might change into a "watchful part." We use these examples to illustrate how bringing Self into the leadership can help parts shift from out-of-balance states to states which allow them to perform their natural function in the system. In later chapters we will describe how parts work can help this transformation take place.

Mindfulness and Self

The purpose of IFS or "parts work" therapy is to bring the Self into the foreground, and we have found that meditation practices from spiritual traditions can also help with this process. One of the most effective practices is the Buddhist practice of "mindfulness" which is similar to the state of consciousness we call Self. In our visits to museums and temples around the world, we have found that representations of the Buddha

in a state of centered meditation convey the essence of the Self. For this reason
we have chosen to offer this image of a quiet inner smile as another way of
representing the qualities of Self.

**When we are
on the level of
the Self, we can
smile at our parts,
seeing them with
compassion and
understanding.**

Mindfulness can bring a peaceful and observing awareness to the actions
of everyday life. One can walk with mindful awareness, prepare dinner with
peaceful awareness, wash the dishes, or answer the phone
with awareness. In terms of parts work, we would say
that we are going about these daily tasks of life
with the Self in the center of the living room.

Research has shown the health benefits
of mindfulness, and in recent years its
benefits in psychotherapy have also been
studied. Even cognitive behavioral therapists,
known for their research-based, rational
approach to therapy, have embraced the use of
mindfulness meditation because of the powerful effect
it has in helping people to find a peaceful calm center from
which to live their lives.

A personal experience of mine illustrates the power of these mindfulness
practices. I was at a week-long retreat focused on Buddhist psychology with
Thich Nhat Hanh at Plum Village in France. As part of the retreat we were
divided into small groups to do the mindfulness working practices which are
part of Thich Nhat Hanh's retreats. My small group included a number of
professors like myself, as well as other psychologists from around the world and
several monks. I was looking forward to the daily mindfulness work practice.

In my mind I could see myself peacefully chopping vegetables or digging
in the garden. When we received the working meditation assignment it was

not one of these imagined activities but rather to clean the toilets for the 600 people at the retreat for the whole week. The mindfulness practice began before I even started the task, as I became aware of my automatic aversion to what one finds in dirty toilet areas.

Using the mindfulness practice, centering in Self, I honored my "grossed out" part for letting me know I should be careful here for health hazards. I also became aware that waste products leaving our body are a natural part of life that doesn't need to be reacted to with such aversion. I became aware that when seen from Self, I could see my job for what it was. By cleaning this area we would give many others ease and joy at having a clean toilet space which they could use. (That doesn't mean the "grossed out" part was no longer there; it was just more in the background.)

Our group ended up singing and joyfully cleaning the toilets every day. To our surprise, we had transformed an aversive response into a peaceful, joyful practice. That, in itself, would have made the practice very worthwhile, but what happened afterwards showed me that such a practice can have a profound effect on how I respond to other difficult situations.

On the last day of the retreat I received a phone call that my father had had a heart attack and that I needed to get home as soon as possible. As I flew home I felt the fear of losing my father, but I also found myself centered enough to be able remember how much I loved him. I felt gratitude for what he had brought to my life. When I got home I was thankful he was still alive. Together as a family we had to discuss difficult decisions about surgery, the risks and benefits. I experienced a capacity to be present and calm through the whole process.

At one point someone remarked that it was too bad that the benefits of my retreat had to be lost because of such an upsetting event. I remember realizing that the opposite was true, that the retreat had been a perfect preparation for this experience. The toilet cleaning meditation strengthened my access to Self in the midst of crisis.

In the following chapters we will describe how and why parts develop as they do, how they can become extreme and the various ways we can bring Self into the living room and help parts transform into their natural form and function. Dialog with them through parts work makes it possible for the Self to assume a leadership role. In addition, there are many ways to support the Self as we move through everyday life. One of the simplest is to do things that help you to be aware of your parts. By reading this book, becoming mindfully aware of your parts as they arise in your everyday life, noticing what they do for you and by doing the exercises at the end of the chapters, you can strengthen the Self in your system.

Simple awareness exercises such as meditation and mindfulness practices taught in Buddhism and other traditions are ways to strengthen the Self. Thich Nhat Hanh calls them "watering the seeds of mindfulness." One method is sitting and simply being aware of breathing in while breathing in, and breathing out while breathing out. You will find a guide to this practice at the end of the chapter. It is simple but powerful practice because it takes only a few moments and you can do it any time during the day. It is a direct way of exercising the Self, much as you would use sit ups to strengthen your abdominal muscles. A little bit every day adds up.

While the goal of these practices is to help ourselves be in the centered state of Self, there is a danger that we may get the idea that we should somehow find ourselves in a constant state of peace, of calm, of Self. Given human nature, none of us will be living constantly in a state of Self. The reality is that most of the time our consciousness bounces around from parts to the Self, from less aware to more aware and back again, but the Self can become increasingly available as we exercise our awareness.

Mindful Breathing
Exercising Self Through
Awareness of the Breath

The Basic Practice:

- Find a comfortable place to sit which doesn't have a lot of distractions.

- You can sit on a chair, a meditation cushion or bench—whatever is most comfortable for you.

- A key is to have your spine comfortably erect and your head balanced. This posture helps you to become relaxed without becoming distracted or going to sleep.

- Make a few deep exhalations, stretch and move further into a comfortable position.

- Direct your attention to the breath:

  o Observe the sensation of the air moving in and out through the nose.

  o Allow your breath to move naturally: you simply observe it.

  o Notice the sensations associated with breathing, the rise and fall of your belly, the air moving in and out of your nose.

  o Notice how it feels as you begin the inhalation, how it feels as you are between the inhalation and the exhalation; notice the sensations of the breath on the exhalation.

o   When thoughts and feeling arise, observe them without
    judgment, from Self, and let them go. Your parts will
    certainly enter the open space in your living room and begin
    to distract you from concentrating on your breath. Simply
    smile at them and return your attention to your breath.

Getting into Self:

At moments during the day when you think of it, stop what you are
doing for a minute, take three deep breaths and return to awareness,
to Self. Some routine events can be signals for moving back from
your parts and toward the Self. For instance, Thich Nhat Hanh
suggests that when the phone rings you breathe three times before
answering it. You can turn many routine events into opportunities to
remember Self, such as getting into the car, turning the ignition key,
stopping at a red light, or unlocking the front door. These can also be
signals to stop, take a moment and step back into Self.

Mindfulness of Parts:

* During your everyday activity you might bring your attention to
  the parts as they arise

* When you notice a particular state of mind associated with a
  part, you might smile at that part of yourself and say something
  like "Hello worry, I notice you are active today." Simply
  acknowledging a part with compassion can return you to Self.

* If the part is strong and seems to need attention, you might have
  an inner dialogue with the part to find out what makes it so active
  at this time.

Chapter 3

How Parts Develop
"Parts is Parts"

As we grow up, many things determine which parts will become stronger in our internal system. We are born with physical and temperamental characteristics, and to these are added life experiences that cause certain parts to become more active. In this chapter we'll take a look at some of these developmental processes.

All of our parts arise to help us adapt to physical, psychological and social needs. This helping function is what we call the positive intention of each of our parts. Each part originally developed to help the system even when its behavior seems negative. This positive intention can sometimes be difficult to see when what we notice is the self-destructive nature of some behavior. It is also hard to keep in mind that another person's parts have a positive intention when their behavior is annoying or hurting us.

As we developed into who we are now, the parts that are our major players gradually took on their shape and form. Some parts received a lot of support while others were discouraged from appearing. Let's take a look at the range of parts we develop as we move from early childhood survival and development to adult coping strategies.

Physical and Survival Parts

Some of our parts are there to ensure our very survival. One of the survival needs we have is food. So it makes sense that a powerful part in our system is the part that takes over the living room when we are hungry and says, "Hey, it's time to eat and I have some ideas about what would taste good." We have named this part the "happy pig." This happy pig part takes great joy in being employed as the monitor of hunger: its job is to recognize when we are hungry, to know what tastes good, to find it, eat it and enjoy it.

Some of our parts, like the happy pig, help us take care of our physical needs.

Other parts related to the survival of the species have to do with our system's response to others: for example, the nurturing part of ourselves involved in childrearing. It is critical that the mother respond to the cues from a baby with a nurturing response.

If the maternal part cannot be brought into the living room when needed, growth and even survival is very difficult for the infant. It is vital that our systems can respond to the situation with the part of ourselves needed to best manage the situation we are in. For that reason, humans and especially women are chemically programmed to respond strongly to the stimulus conditions presented by the birth of a baby. The hormones can have a powerful effect on what parts are available. A psychologist friend who was very committed to her professional identity said when she became pregnant that she would have the child and be back to work in a few weeks.

If we are identified with our professional roles, the manager parts are often prominent in our living room.

She was not under family or social pressures to be a stay-at-home mom. Her professional parts were clearly the main cast of characters in her living room. However, the biological processes which occurred after the child was born changed things completely.

She absolutely fell in love with the baby and did not want to do anything else but be with him. Her professional parts had a hard time finding space in her living room. She did not go back to work for some time.

For the survival of babies it is critical that the nurturing parts of the parents are activated.

Fortunately for babies, the hormones designed to activate a caring response from the mother will make caring for the child a priority in its system, so that the maternal parts take up much of the space in the "living room" during the early months. This doesn't always work flawlessly, of course: instances such as postpartum depressions are examples of where the physiological state actually works against the availability of the nurturing part.

Another survival part is our fear part. This part is on the lookout for physical or social dangers we might be facing. What would happen if we didn't have sufficient parts on the lookout for danger? One clear example for me is when, as a teenager, I visited New York City with some friends in the 1960s. Through a combination of ignorance and being teenage boys our

fear parts were not active; thus we went wandering through Central Park at 1:00 in the morning having a great time. This was not a safe thing to be doing, since many muggings and even murders were occurring in Central Park at that time. Our fear parts should have been more active.

If our frightened or careful parts aren't activated when they need to be we can put ourselves in dangerous situations.

You can bet that had my mother known about this, her worry parts would have been going full bore, and her protective parent parts would never have let us travel again without her spending a great deal of time trying to activate our fear parts so we wouldn't do such a stupid thing again. Fortunately, life can be forgiving and many teenage boys survive escapades that would cause their mother's "worry parts" to make her hair stand on end.

When our fear part is operating effectively it notices danger and activates our fight or flight response. This response has the strong biological component of the adrenal hormone release, which raises the arousal level of the system. In this activated state we have the energy to run or to fight. If the fight response dominates, then the anger part could almost immediately take over the living room.

Fight, freeze or flight are three parts which might be activated when we are frightened.

Anger gives us the energy to protect ourselves. While this raw energy was useful in primitive societies for the fighting process, if it takes over the living room in present times, we often lose judgment and do things that hurt ourselves and others. In a later chapter we will look at how anger can be transformed from a rage state to its optimal protective and boundary-setting role.

Parts that Help us Adapt

While hunger, fear and anger are related to our physical survival, we also have other parts whose function as we grow is to help us succeed in our social world. Early in life there are responses by the baby which activate the parents' caretaking parts. Initially aimed at keeping the nurturing parts of the parents involved to ensure survival of the infant, they are internalized into the mind of the child and shape the character of what we call approval-seeking parts.

Parts which want to please others are important for coming into right relationship to our environment.

Meanwhile, the parents are busy trying to develop the self-regulatory parts of the child so she can go to the toilet in the toilet, eat at dinner time, sleep when it is time to sleep and play when it is time to play. From these parental responses to the child's behavior, internal parts develop in the child: manager parts who know what is safe to touch and what is not, what you can say and what you can't say, what is "good" and what is "bad," what makes you a "good child," and what makes you a "bad child."

Out of these years of interactions arise parts that take on the lessons from those experiences and become judging, critical or moralistic parts in the person's internal system.

These parts are similar to what Eric Berne in Transactional Analysis called "critical parent" ego states, and they also have similarities to Freud's "superego." The critical and judging parts developed in order to help us get approval from others. This group of parts has learned the expectations of the outer world and now gives those messages to the inner system without any outside activation.

These critical and judging parts are often protecting vulnerable parts that are easily hurt if we perceive ourselves as criticized or rejected by others. These vulnerable child parts are easily embarrassed or shy.

Inner critics have internalized the expectations of the world around us, and try and protect our vulnerable parts through self criticism.

To balance out the critical and judging parts, most systems have a rebel part that fights against the inner and outer critics and judges. These rebel parts are particularly strong during adolescence. What is their function?

Rebellious parts assert our autonomy and support the development of our individual identity.

Whereas the inner critic and judge have the function of helping the person to adapt to the family and social norms, the rebel part has the function of pushing against parental and social expectations so that the person can develop autonomy and individual identity.

Manager Parts

As we grow up, parts called managers develop. The functions of these parts are to assess the needs and capacities of the system, to accurately interpret the demands and the conditions of the external context and to develop a plan of action to best meet internal and external conditions. A good example of a manager part is the multitasker:

This part helps us get done what needs to be done. With the large number of roles that must be filled in today's world, especially by women, many people need this part in the living room to help manage their many internal and external demands.

The multi-tasker helps us to manage all of the complex tasks of modern life.

Managers can take on many forms: for example, a list maker helps to prioritize tasks. Other manager parts organize other people, reminding them of what must be done. The woman on the right could be called the delegator.

The priority manager loves to make "to do lists," so we can organize our day.

The delegator helps us organize others to do the tasks that need to be done.

These managers compete with each other and a wide range of other parts for space in our living room. Our family, social tasks and personal needs each demand time and space. The dynamics of today's social and economic systems require people to juggle rapidly many tasks. The living rooms of people's systems are filled with parts jockeying for time and energy to meet the demands of internal and external conditions. The statements below represent some of the external demands that can activate various manager parts.

We see, then, that there is a wide array of parts designed to help us cope with the tasks of living. Our mental software is indeed sophisticated. It actually writes itself as we grow up to fit the context we live in. We can find the origin of our major parts in key events in our development, and they shape our inner system. A family crisis or our role in the family influences the development of our parts as does the social context.

These drawings of parts are meant to reflect forms that people may discover as they visualize their parts. Therapists who explore the inner system find that each client has a different way of experiencing or imaging her parts. This aspect of parts work is one of the creative and interesting things about the work: the client and therapist discover the parts as each individual moves along the path of discovering their own inner system. One of the exercises that I have my students do is to generate a map of their own internal system. At the end of this chapter you will find an outline of steps for developing such a map yourself. I have included examples of ways various people have approached representing their inner world of parts.

Parts Map Exercise

1. Look at examples of the parts maps on the next pages and at your notes from the exercise in chapter 1. You may use these ideas to begin planning a parts map.

2. Create images in the way that works best for you. You could make a collage, using pictures from magazines or other sources of images such as http://images.google.com/. You could also draw or paint your own images or simply write out the names and characteristics of your parts in a diagram format.

3. You can use the types of parts discussed in this chapter or other parts that you find are aspects of your inner system. Some people find a lot of parts while others have only a few.

4. Arrange these images in a configuration that best expresses your inner world. You might place parts near each other if they go together and you might in some way show parts which are in conflict. You can vary the size and placement of the images to reflect the amount of space they take up in your system. Feel free to use whatever form works best for you.

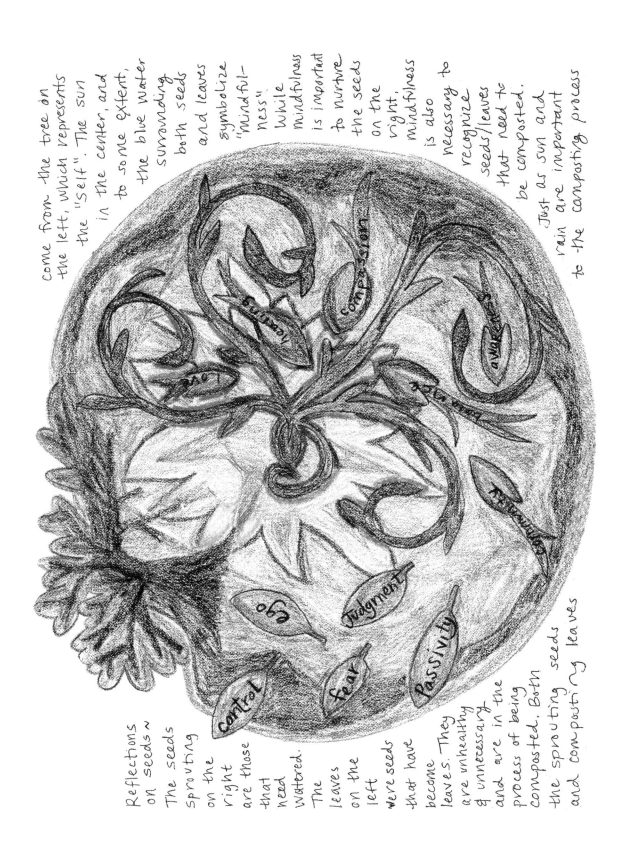

come from the tree on the left, which represents the "self". The sun in the center, and to some extent, the blue water surrounding both seeds and leaves symbolize "mindful-ness" while mindfulness is important to nurture the seeds on the right, mindfulness is also necessary to recognize seeds/leaves that need to be composted. Just as sun and rain are important to the composting process

Reflections on seeds ~ The seeds sprouting on the right are those that need watered. The leaves on the left were seeds that have become leaves. They are unhealthy & unnecessary and are in the process of being composted. Both the sprouting seeds and composting leaves

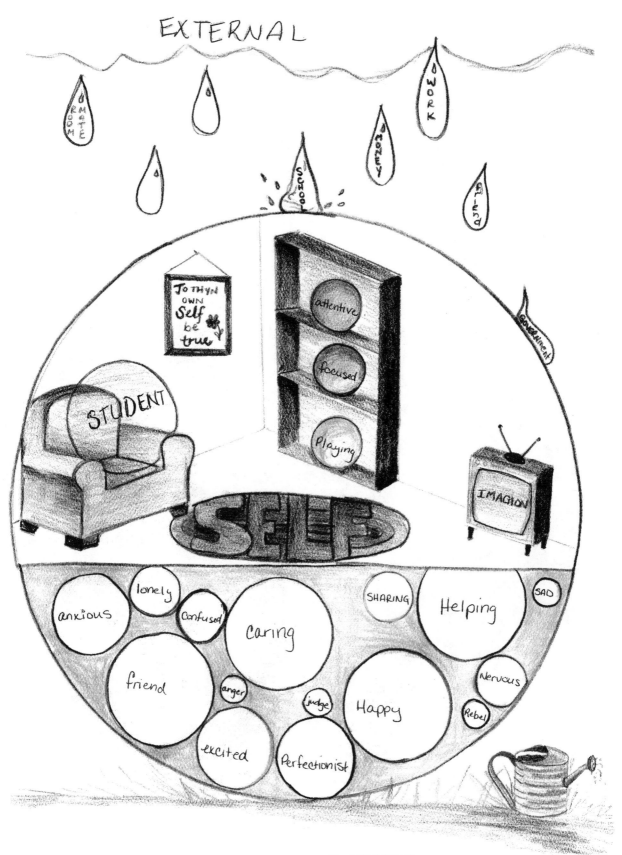

EXTERNAL

Chapter 4

How the Parts Interact
"Then another part of me says . . ."

We have noticed that there often are several parts in the living room of our mind vying for attention. In doing parts work therapy we have discovered that when problems take a lot of time to unravel, it is often because there are groups of parts that are polarized or in coalition with other parts. Identifying and working with these dynamics within the system are important steps in bringing the system into balance. Here is a light-hearted example of conflicts and coalitions that might appear in our lives.

The Happy Pig part takes great joy in being employed as the caretaker of hunger: its job is to find food and to enjoy eating it. Its first salvo into our consciousness may be to make us aware of hunger pangs, or perhaps, if it is a very alert Happy Pig, to send us images of some food we enjoy before hunger pangs even arise. "Why wait?" is the Happy Pig's motto. It may be that Happy Pig takes over without ever announcing itself in our mind: it simply slides open our desk drawer and we find ourselves licking our lips after eating the Twinkie or the brownie stored there earlier.

A part whose job is to look for enjoyment can use clever strategies to get it.

This strategy on the part of Happy Pig has the advantage of not waking up opposing coalition parts: the inner food critic, the health trainer, the body image manager, and the Judge.

In many people there is a coalition of parts who try to keep the person fit and healthy.

This is a group of parts that Happy Pig has labeled the Privy Council of food intake. This crew, the Happy Pig feels, is better left sleeping. The Happy Pig's point of view is, "Look, we know you are going to end up eating that Twinkie anyway, it was a done deal when you brought it to work, so why go through all of those inner machinations first?"

Despite the Happy Pig's opinion to the contrary, the Privy Council might lodge a formal protest to the Self-Improvement Manager. It may be that this person has recently been taking a holistic health class on healthy choices, so this part is in the foreground. The Council objects to the habit they have observed in which a Twinkie is eaten every afternoon without letting the Privy Council have input into the decision.

One of the ways the Council works is to get our attention when we look in the mirror, step on the scales or perhaps see an article about healthy nutrition in the paper. They then harangue us with feelings of guilt and remorse for being such an ignorant slob and eating Twinkies. To appease these parts, our Self-Improvement Manager suggests something like putting a sticky note on the Twinkie package which says "Think!" That way we could have input from various concerned parts and delay eating the Twinkie. This delay lasts for about twenty minutes, at which point when the Privy Council has its back turned the Happy Pig returns, and the person ignores the sticky note and eats the Twinkie.

The Privy Council takes note of this devious action and wants a more effective plan for interrupting this automatic pattern. The person might go to a behavior management counselor, and the Privy Council is happy to agree with some of her suggestions. The Council decides it would be more effective to interrupt the cycle earlier in the process, ideally at the point when the Twinkie is being purchased at the store or at least when it is being packed to take to work. This plan would "guarantee" that eating a Twinkie at work stops.

However, be forewarned that the Happy Pig is very persistent and creative. Given that you now have no Twinkie in your drawer it is likely that you will find yourself wandering down the hall to the lunchroom where frequently someone has deposited the leftover donuts from an earlier meeting. While your workplace manager part is in the living room discussing important issues with a colleague, thus keeping the Privy Council from coming into the living room, Happy Pig will quietly consume two glazed donuts. Who knows? If the work discussion was intense enough, reports may never reach the Privy Council of this infraction, thus avoiding any annoying gnashing of teeth and bitter recriminations being levied at the Happy Pig.

The internal systems view of the personality explains why these "behavioral management" efforts did not work and this pattern did not change. The situation did not change because the polarization between the Happy Pig and the Privy Council was never addressed and there was no true negotiation between them. To break this cycle Happy Pig needs to be part of the solution, not sabotaging the process. For this to happen the person needs to move into Self, and then to enter into a true dialogue about nutrition with the Happy Pig, perhaps giving it the job of planning tasty nutritious snacks, with the Privy Council giving input on nutrition and exercise. We will explain the process of this type of dialogue in chapter 5.

Parts Coalitions

Alliances among parts like the one we saw with the Privy Council are common in the internal system. These alliances or coalitions are groups of parts that have shared perspectives and goals for the system. These groups of parts tend to be activated together and can have a dominating presence, taking over the living room of our consciousness. Discovering and working with such a coalition was an important part of my own inner work.

An overly active coalition of helping parts can take over the living room and lead to the person's becoming burned out.

When I began my own parts therapy, my focus was on the fact that during my early years as a therapist I often felt on the verge of burnout. When I

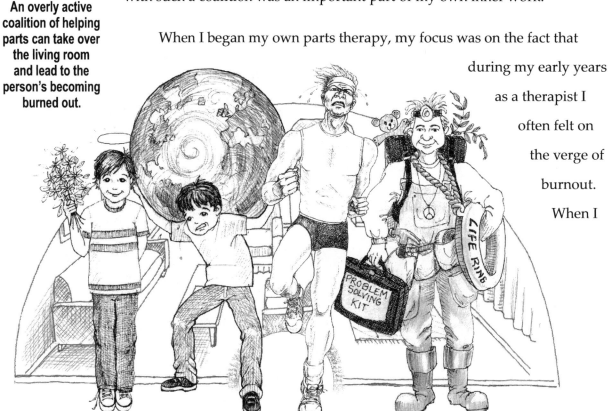

began to work with my parts I found that in my system I had a very powerful coalition of parts that were contributing to my burnout. This coalition had a little boy part who wanted to do what was good and helpful, and another little boy part who felt responsible and burdened: there was also a well developed helper part with a lot of resources and a part I called Steel.

Steel knew no pain and was never tired. He was the part of me that at the weight of one hundred twenty-five pounds was the all-conference football defensive back in high school; he was the part of me that ran marathon races; and he was the part of me that could push me as a therapist, activist and family member until I was completely exhausted and not even know it.

Sometimes young parts carry burdens for years that are much too heavy for them.

The parts work for my system focused on separating out this coalition and finding out what had caused it to drive me so. Separating Steel out and dialoging from the Self went quite smoothly. He was happy to have another assignment; helping me to get tenure and playing hard at racquetball (though he did enjoy the racquetball more). The therapist/helper part was also fairly easy to separate out and understood after years of training and supervision the limitations of what it could do.

The burdened little boy, it turns out, was the pivotal part. He would take on the problems and needs of others as if they were his own to carry and was heavily weighed down by this responsibility. During my therapy I learned that this extreme form of taking on burdens was the little boy's way of coping with the death of my younger sister when I was eleven years old and his way to try and help the family.

The therapy process helped him to set the burdens down. However before he could do this I had to first experience with him the deep grief he still carried about the loss of his sister as well as to sort through feelings of responsibility and guilt that he had developed in his attempt to cope with the experience of her illness and death.

This example is quite typical of how inner systems work. The coalition of parts had developed a rigid and extreme form as a way to help this little boy deal with an extremely difficult experience. In order for them to shift, they had to first step back and be recognized by Self. Then the root cause of the rigid coalition had to be addressed in the therapeutic process. Once the

How we react to others depends on what parts are in our living room when we encounter them.

over-responsible little boy part was unburdened, the other parts could assume a balanced role in the system. I could be helpful without being overly helpful and Steel could give me the determination to push forward when that was needed. My little boy parts could express a wider range of feelings needed for me to have a more balanced life.

Not all coalitions become as problematic as mine. Many parts gather together because they have shared roles and values in the inner system. They become problematic when they are attempting to cope with trauma, and they can get stuck in a rigid forms as they try to help.

In responding to an everyday event it is possible to see how different inner coalitions in the same person react to the same situation. For instance, if you see a beggar panhandling on the street, you can have very different reactions depending on the coalition of parts that is ready to jump into the living room. First let's imagine that you are returning from church, temple or a political awareness meeting after hearing a talk on caring for the poor. This circumstance predisposes you to having certain parts nearer to the surface of the living room. It is not surprising that the helping part is activated and comes into the living room with a whole coalition of parts that support the action of doing something for the beggar.

Here the caring and nurturing parts want to help the homeless person they see on the street.

Notice here that in addition to our well-prepared helper, there is the nurturing part, as well as the good little girl, who all feel good when they are helping. With such a strong helping coalition the person might not just give something to the beggar but spend the next few hours making sure he has shelter and linking him to social services and a jobs program.

Now, instead of just having come from a social awareness event, let's imagine that it is Friday afternoon and you are on your way home, exhausted from a hard week's work with one demand after another having been made on you. Now when you see the beggar a very different cast of characters comes into your living room. In such a situation, when you see the beggar, instantly a bossy manager part is activated and yells, "Get a job, you bum!"

Here we have critical and judging parts in our living room and we might blame the person for getting himself into this condition.

This bossy part has a whole coalition of parts as well. The stern moralist is sure that the beggar has done something to land himself in this situation, the overly judgmental part confirms this and the critical part also has a lot to say.

Let's see what might happen when we get into the Self state of mind. Both teams are in our living room and Self is seeing them as they argue with each other.

When Self is present, both coalitions with their different perspectives can be present at the same time. From this perspective we hear both sides of the argument. Now instead of an automatic response, we may have an internal dialogue to sort out our responses. If we are centered in the Self we are able to listen to the full range of perspectives we have in ourselves and mediate a solution.

Perhaps as a compromise the critics are willing to give the person a small amount of money, "as long as you don't waste your morning helping this guy out, something he surely doesn't want anyway." The helper part can be satisfied with this compromise if you can "smile when you give the money and make respectful contact in the process." This all happens in an instant and we continue down the street, Happy Pig planning what we will order at the restaurant we were on our way to.

If we can get centered in the Self we can consider the perspectives and arguments of all of the parts.

These examples illustrate both the nature of inner coalitions of parts and how we can respond very differently to the same situation depending on what parts the preceding conditions have brought into our living room. Because different parts have different roles, attending to the different needs in our system, it is natural that conflicts will arise as these competing needs and fears are worked out. Bringing the awareness of Self into the process allows us to resolve these conflicts, because being in Self allows input from all our parts.

Inner Coalitions

Looking at your parts map, think about parts that might form a coalition in your inner system.

- Jot down your thoughts about this.

- You might remake your map in such a way as to express the coalitions you are aware of.

- Consider how such a coalition helps you on some occasions or causes you difficulty in other situations.

Chapter 5

Getting the Parts in Balance
*"This part means well,
but it is working way too hard"*

When Parts Work Too Hard

If all of our parts are supposed to function in a positive way for us, why is it that some of them cause so much trouble? Usually because they originated when our system was under stress, they have became overly active: they take up too much space in our living room and appear too often, even when it is not appropriate. Therapy focused on working with the parts takes the client into the Self and has the client dialogue with the parts in order to hear their story and find out why they are doing what they are doing. Once the client understands the positive intention of the parts, the client and therapist can help the part see how what they are now doing is not helping then help the system to come back in balance.

Interestingly enough, parts seem to have minds of their own. Their view of how to help the person's system is sometimes quite limited, usually because they retain beliefs that the person had at an earlier age or under different circumstances. Finding the source of these beliefs can also be an important aspect of helping the system to regain its balance.

Getting to Know our Parts

It has been my experience that there are four dimensions to each part: sensory, emotional, verbal, and imagery. Each of these aspects of the part offers a doorway to understanding and working with the parts. The way the part manifests in the body is the sensory dimension. It might be tension in the neck, a knot in the stomach, or a weight on the shoulders. Becoming aware of how our body feels and reacts in an activating situation can guide us to knowing which part of us is reacting.

The emotional dimension refers to the level of emotions such as fear, anger, joy sorrow, desire, etc. A therapist with good listening skills reflects and clarifies feelings, and this process alone can bring a great deal of relief to people. From a parts work perspective this is because that part of us feels heard and understood. At the same time, by clarifying and becoming aware of our feelings we move more into Self. For example just *being* hurt or anger, that is to say when those parts take up the whole living room with no Self present, is very different than being aware of hurt or angry feelings. Then the Self is present.

The verbal dimension is also called the cognitive dimension. When this aspect of a part is being considered, the client and the therapist explore what the part says or would like to say when it is activated. For example, a client feels hurt after seeing an acquaintance on the street who ignored him. The part that is hurt might be saying that the person doesn't like him. On a day when he feels even more vulnerable, the part might go on to say, "There must really be something wrong with me." The vulnerable child part can easily get caught in such thought patterns.

On the other hand, if the individual were in Self, he might just say, "Hmmm, that person seems very distracted today and didn't even notice me." This verbal dimension of a part is a favorite area for cognitive behavioral therapists to explore. They look for automatic irrational thoughts that arise when we interpret situations in ways that cause us to have negative emotional reactions; the cognitive behavioral therapist challenges them with rational thought. Exploring automatic thoughts and beliefs can also be a dimension of parts work. In parts work, however, it is in the context of trying to understand the distorted belief of a part of the inner systems from the perspective of Self. It is also understood that the cognitive level of a part is only one of its dimensions in the systemic structure. Nevertheless, helping parts let go of the irrational beliefs they carry can be very helpful.

Imagery can also be an important aspect of parts work therapy. When the therapist and client have clarified the thoughts, feelings and sensations that suggest a part, many clients will have a picture come into their mind representing that part. Once the image is there, the therapist guides a dialogue with this internal representation of the parts. This is a dynamic and interesting process but difficult to understand if you haven't actually experienced it. With the therapist helping to structure the process, the parts will often respond with an internal voice or by showing us pictures. One reason for this illustrated book is to offer examples of the imagery dimension of parts for those who haven't had a chance to experience the inner work itself.

In getting to know our parts we can use any one of these four dimensions as the doorway. Many models of therapy focus primarily on one dimension. With the parts work we can start with whichever dimension seems most available and relevant to the parts we are working with, keeping in mind that by looking at other dimensions we might get a deeper understanding of the part. Our experience has been that when the client is able to use imagery the inner work progresses more rapidly.

Exploring Parts

To illustrate this inner process we will explore a common emotion that can cause people difficulty, anger. Sometimes people come to therapy because they find themselves "losing it" with others or fuming at any provocation or having difficulties with a child or a partner because their anger flares up too quickly.

Since anger is usually a strong feeling, the emotional dimension is already clear. The therapist might explore the sensory dimension: how the body feels when the client is angry. Is it a clenched jaw or fist, a racing heart? Then the question might be, "What does this 'clenched fist part' want to say or do?" Then the therapist might ask what that part would look like if it had a form. Sometimes this will be a human form, sometimes an object such as a cloud or, in the case of anger, often a fire or a red ball. Here we see a picture of anger in an extreme form.

After the part has taken some form, the therapist asks the client to imagine that the part separates a little so that client can get to know it better. One client imagined looking at a part something like this representation of anger. The client's reaction might well be, "Help! Get me away from him!" That would be a scared part reacting. With the inner work we would ask the client to become aware of her scared part and what it might look like. Often with this type of reaction it is a frightened child part, but we are open to whatever arises in the person's system and try not to speculate or put our ideas or associations into what this part might be.

Rage is a protector part in extreme form, activated when a person feels threatened.

The next step would be to have the client imagine being present with but separate from the frightened child part, perhaps by finding a safe place for the child to be. At this point we would ask how the client felt toward the child. If the reaction was a Self quality such as compassion or curiosity the therapist knows that the person is in Self. Then it is possible to proceed by getting to know the parts better with the Self leading the process.

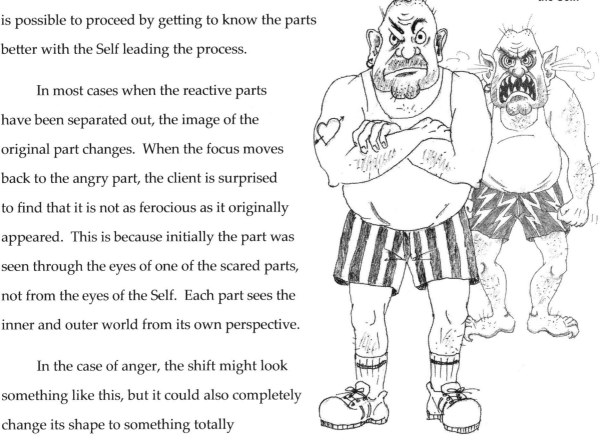

More effective protection comes when the part can take on a more balanced form with the help of the Self.

In most cases when the reactive parts have been separated out, the image of the original part changes. When the focus moves back to the angry part, the client is surprised to find that it is not as ferocious as it originally appeared. This is because initially the part was seen through the eyes of one of the scared parts, not from the eyes of the Self. Each part sees the inner and outer world from its own perspective.

In the case of anger, the shift might look something like this, but it could also completely change its shape to something totally different. One of the wonders of this work is that each person's parts show up in unique ways. It is important not to have preconceived notions of what the part should look like or what it means for the other person.

One of the hardest things in training therapists in this model is to keep them from interpreting the meaning of a client's parts. That is up to the client to do; the therapist's job is to help the person to get into Self and then assist the Self to understand the parts.

What the therapist does is help the person begin to dialogue with the part. The questions asked of the part might be: Why is the part doing what it is doing? What is its job? Does it have a story to tell? It is important with a protective part to ask what it is afraid would happen if it stopped doing what it was doing. In the case of anger, that part is usually convinced that if it didn't flare up the person would be taken advantage of. The angry part usually developed at a time when the person was vulnerable and the anger was a form of self protection. The problem, of course, is that situations change, but often our parts keep reacting in the way they learned to react earlier in life.

After working with the anger part and helping it let go of its extreme position, the client, now more often in the Self, can help the angry part do its job more effectively, so that it protects, draws boundaries, and maintains safety rather than exploding.

Calling on Parts to Help Parts

Sometimes when we are angry we are not able to fully get into the Self because the situation is too activating. We can, in these situations, use a strong and balanced manager part to help us to contain our anger. We feel the anger boiling in us, but we are able to hold ourselves back, keeping from doing something that we would later regret and that would make the situation worse. This is an illustration of one client's use of an effective manager to hold back anger.

Even if we can't get into Self, sometimes a manager part can hold back rage so we don't do something we would later regret.

Protector Parts

What form the protectors take varies from person to person.

As children we are all vulnerable and therefore we develop protective parts as a defense. The anger part mentioned earlier is often a protective part, but there are many other forms that protective parts can take.

These protective parts are almost always protecting a frightened Child Part.

It is for this reason that you can't move a protector out of the living room by attacking it or trying to diminish it in some way. You will only make it more determined to protect the vulnerable parts. The way to get a protector to step back is first to let it know you value its role in protecting the system and then to educate it about resources the person has that they didn't have when the person was a child, which is the point where most protector parts

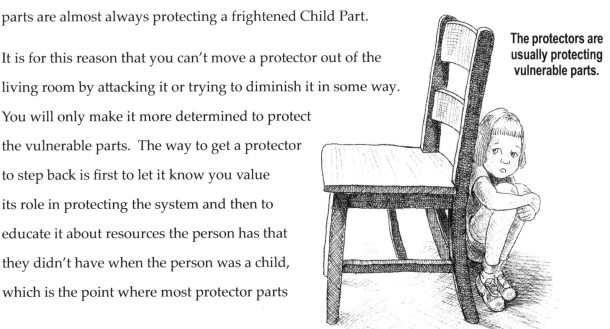

The protectors are usually protecting vulnerable parts.

developed. Helping the protectors learn about and trust the Self is a key part of helping them understand that there are other, more effective, ways to make the system safe and strong. It is surprising, but these parts are able to find better ways of helping once they have been heard in dialogue between Self and part, and they begin to trust the Self and allow it to lead.

Often we see people who have a protective part that always arises when someone tries to get close to them. They fear they might be hurt, and armor themselves for protection. This can have a chilling effect on relationships since it is not comfortable to hug a knight in full armor. We often hold on to the psychological armor that we developed after we were hurt as children, even though we now have all the resources of an adult. We have more control over our situation now and adult judgment about who is safe and not safe. The result of having these rigid protectors in our adult life may be that we keep people away through various maneuvers, making it very difficult to have the kind of relationships we desire.

Inner protectors make sure that no one gets too close, putting vulnerable parts at risk.

Protector parts can use many other behaviors such as being aloof or unfriendly with coworkers or friends, adopting a "tough guy" stance, or dominating the conversation at every opportunity. A client of Lauri's had trouble because she was typically irritable and impatient with people at work and home. Thus her relationships were always strained. She looked for the part that had this defensiveness and found a very fierce, wild alley cat. She managed to visualize putting the cat in a small safe room and asked it what it would need to moderate its fierceness. The cat told her that she would have to "visit" it in her mind every day and maybe then, the cat said, it would begin to trust the client. This client's former therapist, on hearing of this image said, "That's perfect! This woman was basically thrown out into the alley as a child, rejected by her own family and in a series of foster homes."

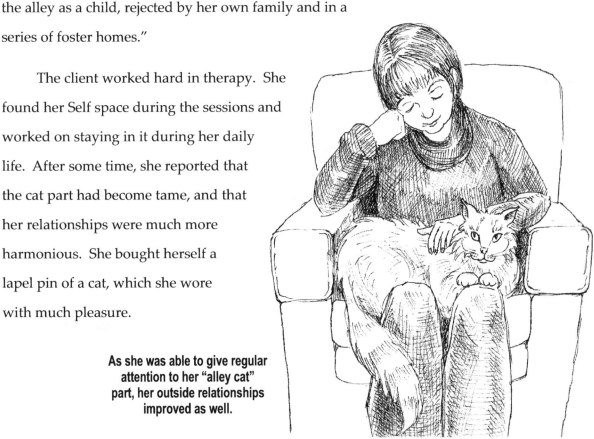

A woman who was always in a permanent protective stance in relationships found an inner "alley cat" protector part.

The client worked hard in therapy. She found her Self space during the sessions and worked on staying in it during her daily life. After some time, she reported that the cat part had become tame, and that her relationships were much more harmonious. She bought herself a lapel pin of a cat, which she wore with much pleasure.

As she was able to give regular attention to her "alley cat" part, her outside relationships improved as well.

Another of Lauri's clients was a very tall, large man who often had a hard scowl on his face. He was having considerable difficulty in relationships because people were so threatened by his size and manner. As a child he had been mercilessly beaten by his father and so he lived in a constant state of fear. In therapy, he found a "Tank Part" that was protecting him. The therapy work involved slowly working him into the position of driving the tank, instead of just letting it run over people.

Though it shouldn't have surprised Lauri or the client, one day the top of the tank opened and out popped a frightened little boy. It was now safe for him to come out and be cared for. Through the therapeutic process the client was in fact able to get control over much of his life and he was less defensive in relationships as the Self became more and more available and his parts less extreme.

People with strong protective parts armoring them usually have a wounded and vulnerable child inside.

Critics, Judges and Boss Parts

Critical or judging parts can become too strong in our systems because of childhood experiences in learning what we should and shouldn't do. Taking in our parents' admonitions about what is permissible and what is not, we gradually develop our own inner judges that remind us of the social rules of our family and community. It is of course vital that we develop these parts, for later they will help us learn how to be successful within our social context. It is, however, easy for our system to get out of balance in this process.

A complicating factor is that our biological predisposition causes each of us to learn differently, depending upon the temperament we were born with. The difference between the introverted and the extroverted child is a good example. One effect of this temperamental difference is that introverts are much more reactive to external stimuli, such as the stern voice of the parent. If we apply that difference to the process of developing our inner critics and judges we find this temperamental difference can have a strong impact.

Take as an example the parent saying no no to a child, perhaps as they were about to touch an object at Grandma's house. The same tone of voice by the parent for the introverted child is heard as **NO NO** while for the extroverted child it is no no, simply because of the difference in the inborn arousal level of their systems. The result of this might be that the introverted child will not touch that or any other object at Grandma's and is made very cautious by the "severe" reprimand. The no no for the extroverted child, on the other hand, barely registers, and two minutes later he is touching the object again.

It is possible under these conditions that the critical and judging parts of the sensitive child may become both harsh and powerful in the system, as the child grows up. This can lead to the development of a severe self-critic

Perfectionism is usually an indication of powerful inner critics and judging parts.

part which keeps the adult in constant fear of being criticized. This can take up much of the person's internal system's energy and create an over-controlled and perhaps perfectionistic system that might look something like this living room with its extreme inner critic and judging parts.

The extroverted child may have underdeveloped inner critics and judges, even though the parents' response was the same to each child. This can result in difficulties as the extroverted child interacts with their social environment.

If the person has not internalized external norms enough, the person will find themselves struggling with those around them.

His inner system might look like this illustration, where the critical and judging parts are very small and barely get into the living room. The ideal, of course, would be the image seen in the third picture, where the inner critics and judges are in a healthy form and Self is in a leadership role.

Ideally, through access to the Self, the various parts are able to find their natural and balanced form.

We have traced the development of inner judges and critics. As we have noted, some people internalize the critics to such an extent that they can never accept their own imperfections or those of others. This illustration shows how one client's "moralist" transformed from a harsh, rigid judging stance to a softer, more compassionate moral guide once it was able to shift from its extreme form and when Self was in leadership.

The one is hard, constricted and critical; the other offers a hopeful vision of what the person might become.

When centered in Self, an inner moralistic part can take on a more loving and kind form.

Transforming Critic, Judge and Boss Parts

We saw a friendly manager part in chapter three. This manager was originally a yelling, driving boss part that changed into a more helpful manager-boss part after a dialogue with the Self. When the original Boss Part with the megaphone was asked what his job was, he said that if he did not yell constantly at the client, the client would fall into inactivity and never get anything done. When the client's Self was put in charge and reassured the Boss Part that his concerns were heard, and his fears worked with, he took on a new role as a planner. He took on the task of making lists, becoming a part that many of us could find useful.

All of these parts are problematic when they are working too hard. They have good intentions. However, they take up too much space in the living room and often won't leave when there needs to be space for other parts. As we have said, it is important to remind the parts that we are not trying to get rid of them, but rather to better understand them through dialogue with the Self. That process may take a long time and usually involves finding other parts that are in coalition with or opposition to the problematic part. The work is to let each of the parts have their say.

For instance, one client who was going through a divorce found a dumpy, whiny fourteen-year-old girl part who, she reported, "none of the other parts like." The client really didn't want to talk to this part at first. However, as she was assisted in moving into the Self during the therapy session, she was able to have a dialogue with her. This was the part of her that felt her whole world would collapse when her marriage ended. A year later, coming back for a check-up session, the client said, "I never would have gotten through the divorce so well if I hadn't found that fourteen-year-old girl."

Therapeutic work can help the parts to release their extreme stance and allow them to find their more effective, balanced form.

When Good Parts Become Too Good

People in the helping professions often find themselves with a highly motivated helping part.

Sometimes a part has started out as a very positive attribute. The person has gotten a lot of approval from other people for doing what this part does, but the part gradually takes up more and more of the person's life, taking over the living room and using all of the person's energy. In the case of many helping professionals, it is a helper part.

Such a part may have started out in a central but balanced role in the system with a lot of ability and resources. However, it sometimes happens that the part can become all-encompassing, giving rise to the kind of rescuer part we see here.

These parts can become extreme, taking much of the person's energy and leading to burnout.

Helping professionals who attend my workshops often come with this overactive Helper Part, and they are able to move into a new and more balanced relationship with these parts.   This work is one focus of my "Healing the Healer" burnout prevention workshops.

Worry Parts

Another frequent visitor for many is worry. When it becomes extreme, worry takes up a lot of the living room. It prevents other parts from being there, even though these other parts are needed to judge what is a true danger. These anxious parts can also prevent useful managers from making a plan that will help us cope with possible problems. In its functional form, as we see in this illustration, the part that worries can look ahead and warn us of possible dangers. This can activate the needed parts, but it doesn't exhaust the entire system and keep us awake at night.

Lauri experienced an interesting transformation of a worry part during a mini-parts-work-session we had as we were stuck in traffic at the border between Canada and the United States when coming back from a vacation. Lauri liked her job very much but was quite anxious about going back to work after the vacation because many changes were happening at her agency and there was a turbulent, unpredictable atmosphere there. We used the time waiting in line for a parts work session.

Worried parts can become so extreme that they make day to day functioning very difficult and uncomfortable

In a balanced form, the worried part helps us to look forward and warns us of dangers.

Lauri took some slow deep breaths and was becoming well anchored in her Self. Then, when asked to visualize the worry part, Lauri imagined a small, anxious mouse, running around looking for possible dangers. After talking with the mouse about its function and its worries, I suggested putting the mouse in a safe place to let it rest, and Lauri imagined putting it in a basket lined with soft cotton, whereupon the mouse went to sleep. Then I asked if there could be another part that might be more effective in keeping watch for possible problems on the horizon. Lauri said that she was picturing Athena, in her full regalia, standing on a hill overlooking the landscape.

When she returned to the mouse, after putting Athena in charge of keeping watch, she began to laugh. When she finally caught her breath, she said that the mouse not only was asleep but had turned into a stuffed mouse. Lauri noted later that she returned to work much calmer and was more effective. Thinking of Athena now and then was helpful, but even when that specific image wasn't there she felt much calmer than she had before. By becoming aware of her parts and having the appropriate part, "Athena," in the living room when needed, she had more Self available and could deal more competently with the turbulent events at work. When working with parts, then, the goal is not to get rid of problematic parts but to understand their original intention. The inner work can then help the person find ways to approach situations from the Self with input from the relevant parts.

The exercise that follows offers a chance to experience some of this process. Through inner dialogue with our parts we are able to bring more harmony and balance into our system, helping our parts assume their natural roles.

Bringing Balance to Your System

At the end of this book you will find a web site listed where you can find therapists trained in the IFS model who could help you fully engage in the process of balancing your inner system. The following exercise is not designed to address a serious issue for which one might need the help of a therapist, but rather to help you explore adaptive patterns you may have developed that are not optimal. Take what works for you here and leave what doesn't seem to work.

Reflecting on parts that seem to be working too hard:

- Identify a part that you think may be working too hard.

- What kind of thoughts and feelings do you have when this part is in the living room?

- What do you do when you are in this part?

- See if you can imagine what a picture of it would look like.

- As you think of this part, how do you feel towards it?

- If you have a reaction like judgement or fear, then simply notice all of the parts that configure around this issue as you try to understand all of their differing perspectives.

- If you have a curious or compassionate response you can try asking it the questions that follow.

Further Questions:

- What is this part's job?

- What is it afraid would happen if it didn't work so hard?

- If there were other ways to manage the situation would this part be willing to consider that?

- Is there something the part needs from you in order to do that?

- Over the next week or two explore with the part more useful ways you might use its energy.

Chapter 6

Parts and Relationships

" . . . you always . . . you never . . . "

As we interact with others throughout the day, a wide range of parts enter the living room. As we interact with our children, parents, partners and the people we work with, certain parts are regularly called into play. We have called these repetitive processes "loops." Repetitive loops can be positive. We have certain people in our lives with whom we feel a natural warmth or with whom we are continually joking, or with whom we always seem to have deep discussions about life. However, automatic loops can become problematic in our relationships, creating tension or conflict and limiting ways of interacting.

To find examples of repetitive loops that become negative we have only to look at a typical parent-child impasse. The child breaks a rule or does something rude or thoughtless. The parent's judging part begins a long lecture about responsibility. The youngster's rebel part rises into the living room. His resulting sullen attitude causes the parent's judging part to become more moralistic.

The result of course is predictable: the more the parent lectures, the more stubborn and sullen the child gets, thanks to the rebel parts that are

The more scolding from one person, the more resistance from the other: a typical interpersonal loop.

now taking up his whole living room. After these interactions, these parts of both parent and child are at the edge of the living room, ready to go into action at the least provocation. Systemic family therapists have called this process "the more . . . the more . . . " and they spend a lot of time trying to do what we would call getting both the parent and child into the Self in order to calm the parents' judging and the child's rebellious parts. Once this is achieved, other more productive parts can be available.

Another common source of loops is between a boss and an employee. A judging boss can evoke a rebellious or defender part in a subordinate. Subordinates have their own parts, which can intimidate a boss and bring the boss's defender parts into the living room.

Loops in Partner Relationships

Perhaps more than in any other relationship, loops appear in interactions between partners. Interactions can become repetitious, with certain parts appearing over and over. There are often very well-established loops, with one partner's part automatically calling out a part in the other. Some of the most painful interactions seen in any therapist's office occur when the negative loops in a couple's relationship are being played out.

As poetry helped explore the nature of the Self, so we will use a novel to illustrate this type of painful loop between a couple. Leo Tolstoy, who in his writing shows a brilliant understanding of human psychology, illustrates a dysfunctional series of interactions in his novel, Anna Karenina.

Anna's partner, Vronsky, remains late at his club one evening. Though Anna's inner thoughts say she doesn't want to have another fight with him, she always reproached him for such fighting, nonetheless when he comes home, she find herself involuntarily setting up the fight. She asks with a cold angry expression on her face if he was satisfied now that he had stayed at the club so late. He responds coldly that he wanted to do it, and he did, that is what was important. He then tries to reach out to her tenderly. She is glad at his effort to make peace, but feels some strange power of "evil" in herself. This resentful part will not let her respond to his tenderness. Instead of making peace she coldly tells him he always has to be right.

Then she begins to weep, hoping that this will make him pity her. It works, temporarily, but even as they eat supper and engage in superficial conversation, she now sees in his eyes the very hardening resentment she had been attempting to fight in herself. She realizes that the struggle between them has deepened and will continue to get worse at the next encounter. The momentum of this sequence has taken control of them both.

The more Anna's warrior-defender part jabs at Vronsky, the more his superior sounding armored part arises. When her plaintive crying part comes into play, she succeeds in piercing his armor, but at a great cost, since the next time they disagree, Vronsky's armored part will be stronger and will rapidly come into the living room. Her "fighting" part will have to use more piercing comments, and they will be driven even further apart.

The negative impact of loops in couple interaction can be lessened. The more each person can know his or her parts, and can pause to access the Self in the midst of the fray, the better the chances of the loops being interrupted before they become so destructive.

The Z Process

In looking into partner patterns of interaction, we discovered a process that we have come to call the "Z." The Z is a way of charting habitual parts interactions in a relationship. We call it a Z because unlike a loop, it doesn't end up where it began. The sequence when charted looks like a Z, with each part calling out a different reactive part in the other person. When doing workshops on parts work, Lauri and I sometimes role-play couple interactions. Here is Lauri's account of our discovery of Z's during a role play at a recent workshop:

The role play was a case of art imitating life. It began as an exaggeration of the loops triggered by the fact that Tom is introverted, while I'm an extrovert. This means that he recharges by being quiet and I recharge my energy by being with people. So the scene of the role play is a Friday evening after work. I bounce into the house, with my TGIF part in the living room, while he is in his distracter part, quietly and happily reading the newspaper. Here we are, each in our TGIF parts. You can see that the TGIF part of an extroverted female and that of an introverted male and can be quite different.

Different visions of
how the evening will
play out.

From my TGIF part I enthusiastically announce that I've arranged that we will go to dinner and a movie with some friends this evening

Tom's good little boy part who wants to make Lauri happy and his earnest responsible boy part reluctantly say o.k. to this plan. Notice Grumpy in the background.

Then my Manager comes in and I remind him of the picnic scheduled for Sunday

That pushes his accommodating parts out of the way, and in comes Grumpy.

So this was the first stage of the Z process.

Grumpy's job is to protect Tom from overdoing and give him some space for himself. I quickly see from his face that he's not happy, and the Z" goes on.

I move first into my maternal part, asking him if I can get him something coffee, beer, etc.

He responds from Grumpy with a gruff No.

I then go into my whining sad part, "I've worked so hard all week and I really need to get out and enjoy myself . . . I'm just worn out." (rather like Anna!) in hopes of getting a more pleasant and happy part into his living room.

Tom retreats into the distracter part behind the newspaper, Grumpy at his side. The Helper wanted to jump in, but the other parts won't let him take over.

I notice now that all this time there is a judge part inside me, saying to me that I'm selfish and inconsiderate to this perfectly lovely man who just wants to sit and be quiet!

Finally, (to end the skit) I walk around and breathe, getting at least closer to being in Self. And to my surprise, the words that come out of my mouth as I sit down by him are, "I did it again, didn't I?"

Now, though this was a role play, if you've done role plays you know that you really can get into the role, and I had! And I realized that when I spontaneously said, "I did it again," it was much easier to admit my mistakes when I thought of them as a succession of parts. None of them was the whole of me, and that made it easier to get distance from them and come to the situation from my Self. Together we sat down and with each of us in Self we were able to *speak for our parts* from Self. In this mode it was relatively easy to work out a compromise about how we would spend the weekend.

If we are centered in our Self, we can hear all of our parts, and those of the other person.

Tom Reflects on His Experience of the Z Pattern

My first response to Lauri's request, as you can see in the drawing, is an automatic yes from a little boy part who wants others to be happy and the burdened boy part that takes on his shoulders the needs of other people. This doesn't give Grumpy any room to give input about limiting activities and avoiding overload. When reflecting on my parts in this interaction I see the familiar pattern. The part of me that wants to make others happy and the part that feels its job is to carry the burden get into an automatic "yes" response without checking in with the rest of my system. Then when I get exhausted, my Grumpy takes over the living room, making it very difficult to have any good communication. When Lauri's nurturing part couldn't get Grumpy out of the living room, her sad part set off an internal struggle in me with my Helper wanting to jump in. Grumpy wouldn't leave, however, so the distracter part took over again, burying me in the newspaper and putting a halt to communication.

Let's look at the Z at the beginning of the sequence and explore the nature of the parts activated. In the picture of my first response to Lauri's request to go out, the key for me is the parts that automatically appear in the foreground and say yes. It seems that this moment in the interaction is where I could stop the automatic sequence. If I can avoid the quick automatic yes, it gives the system a chance to get into Self and check with other parts which may have an opinion. Actually it is rare that Lauri would make plans that include me without consulting first so there is usually ample time for me to say, "Let me think about it." I can then check in and see how my various parts are reacting. It is good to check in with Grumpy at this point since his job is to let me and others know when I am maxed out and need rest. If he thinks the system needs down time he can let me know. I can then deal with my parts that want Lauri to be happy. They don't like the idea of saying no, but from Self I explain to them that Lauri will be a lot happier in the long run if I get rest and Grumpy doesn't have to take over. I can then talk with Lauri from Self and let her know that it is too much and that I would rather stay home. Some parts are uncomfortable with her obvious disappointment but those parts are surprised to learn of her resilience and notice that in a half an hour she has found other ways to get what she needs out of the evening.

While breaking the loop at the beginning is the ideal time, the automatic nature of the responses means that sometimes we get further down the Z road before I notice. Some times I first notice Grumpy has taken over the living room when I am putting on a tie getting ready to go out, and I notice him staring back at me in the mirror. With enough Self awareness at that point, I could give voice to Grumpy, hopefully from Self, and just let Lauri know that we need to sit down the next day and go over the schedule, and that I need more down time. It is also possible that Lauri could notice that Grumpy was coming into the living room and from Self let me know that this is happening and ask what my needs are at that point. This can happen more easily when she is in Self and realizes that Grumpy is an expression of my overload and not a critic of her. This keeps her own judging part from beating up on her and setting off her other parts in reaction to Grumpy.

After this role play and discussion in my workshops, I suggest that people pair up and help each other to chart out a Z pattern they notice in a relationship. I have people reflect on the different parts that have come up, looking at what in the other person has activated them. I ask them to reflect on what their function is for the person, why they have come into the living room in this situation and how the Z interaction could be interrupted. At a recent workshop one of the participants drew a Z that involved her and her husband. The sequence was this:

She would clean the house with her Multitasker part in charge.

He would do nothing with his Distracter in charge.

After a time, she would get mad. Wolf part would take over, ripping into him for not helping.

He would get defensive; his Protector would send out remarks about her compulsiveness.

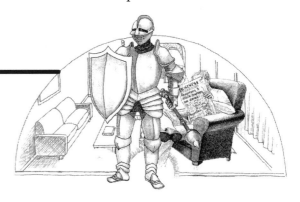

They would arrive at a frosty impasse.

I worked with this person's parts briefly after she described this Z. I found out that the housecleaner part really enjoyed cleaning the house and didn't care so much whether someone helped . . . she enjoyed doing it.

We moved to a dialogue with her angry part. This was the Wolf part who ripped into her husband for sitting around being lazy. As we dialogued with this angry wolf and separated it out, it changed form. When it was seen from Self, it appeared as a puppy.

What looks like a very hostile part can have buried in it a gentle vulnerable part. When we are centered in the Self it can come out.

In dialoging with the puppy, it became apparent that what she wanted was not to have her husband help, but just to be appreciated for her work. Prior to this dialogue she was only aware of her anger and not of her wish for appreciation. It turns out that this angry wolf was protecting her puppy part, which felt vulnerable in her wish for appreciation.

When the participant was able to differentiate the parts of house cleaner and the wolf, she was able to see clearly what she really wanted from her husband. She didn't have much trouble figuring out better ways to get it from him.

What if Anna and Vronsky had access to their parts from Self? Well, maybe there wouldn't have been such a great novel!

Repetitive loops and Z patterns will always be a part of our important relationships. When these Z patterns involve very protective and rigid parts, they become intractable and block out other more constructive ways of working out differences.

The reason that "you always . . . you never . . . " is a watchword among therapists who do relationship counseling is that couples often label each other in a negative way. The parts work view of this process is that one person's protector parts are labeling the other person, usually protecting vulnerable parts of their own system. When these parts can be dialogued with and understood from Self, they are usually able to stop this defensiveness, because they have been heard. In this way we can find safe ways to communicate the needs of these parts to each other.

Exploring Relationship Loops & Z's

Think about a repetitive interaction that you have with another person in your life.

- See if you can identify the parts of yourself that are active in this interaction.

- Can you specifically identify something the other person did or said that activated this part of you?

Reflect on the sequences described in the chapter. Can you identify similar sequences in your own life?

- Think of these reaction sequences in terms of parts in yourself and the other person.

- Try sketching out a Z pattern of these interactions.

- Note: Be cautious about naming other people's parts for them. You might do this for your own understanding, but it is important not to label the other person's parts. Doing this from your protector part is another version of "you always . . . you never . . . " and can lead to destructive communication Z's.

- Think about the function of the parts being activated.

- Reflect on where the sequence could be interrupted by moving into the Self, understanding the parts and speaking for them from Self.

Some parts believe their job is to replay painful situations over and over.

Chapter 7

Distracters and Firefighters
"Holding off the exiles."

How many times during the day do you find yourself turning on the radio when you've already heard the headlines five times, opening the newspaper you've already looked through, eating when you're not hungry, scanning with the remote to find something to watch on TV? As I watch students cross the campus with their iPods[R] or cell phones glued to their ears, I am reminded of how even the open space of walking to class is too much empty living room space for them. Even though we have so much information overload in our modern lives, we race to fill empty space as soon as the stimulation level eases off even a little.

Why is this? From an internal systems perspective these distracters must have some function. At certain times, we are restless. External conditions are not demanding our attention. We want to be free of the inner managers that have been keeping us on task. We want to avoid the constant inner chatter or worry parts, critical perfectionist parts or planning parts that never let us rest. Often the empty space is liable to be filled by ruminations, habitual concerns about work, a relationship issue, this or that worry or aggravation. In the illustration we see a part that one person called "Roma the Ruminator." This part constantly replays situations over and over, reminding us of the pain or fear and hoping for a better outcome this time.

Such ruminators are a common activator of distracter parts. These habitual ruminations can constrict and lock up our system. The distracter parts are a way of moving these parts out of the living room and helping the system to relax. I see them as a kind of screen saver for the psyche. Screen savers were originally developed on computers so that when you leave a typed page on the screen too long it doesn't damage the screen by burning in the patterns left there. If these distracter parts could talk they might say, "Look, if you are going to leave those same old tapes running in your head I'm going to interrupt them with a meaningless but sometimes amusing pattern to put on the TV in the living room of your consciousness."

As soon as someone touches the mouse (i.e. something in the environment demands our attention) this screen saver goes away. Distraction has the function of allowing us to shift gears and to get away from the ruminations of the parts which have been taking up so much space. But when it is there too often and too long, it can keep more useful parts from being accessed.

Exiles

There is another important type of part found in many systems Richard Schwartz calls them exiles. Exiles are parts that for a variety of reasons are not allowed into the living room, and they are often locked away in a part of the store consciousness where they can't be easily activated.

Perhaps these parts were not socially acceptable to our family or friends. One example for boys could be when vulnerable or sensitive parts are punished or shamed by their peer group, father or coach. For girls, the opposite is often true when smart, aggressive or competent parts are punished or at least discouraged by their social surroundings. In such situations manager parts learn to keep these parts safely stored away to avoid the painful social sanctions they fear would occur.

There is another group of Exile parts that are locked away because they carry pain and the memory of traumatic experiences. Manager parts repress these pain-carrying parts and do everything they can to keep these parts from being activated because they fear that the living room would be flooded by the painful memories and feelings.

One of the costs of this strategy is that a manager must always stay in the living room, vigilant that nothing activates the exiled parts. The Self, which carries awareness, is not allowed to take a central role in the system for fear that with awareness will come a flooding of the pain carried by one of the exiles. Despite the manager's best efforts, however, it frequently happens that life circumstances trigger the exiles and they begin to flood the person with pain.

With great effort, manger parts keep exiled parts far from the living room in order to avoid being flooded by the pain they carry.

When Distracters become Firefighters

As we have said, the normal function of a distracter is often to block out pain of some sort. But in the case of exiles, the pain is so great that an

Self-destructive firefighter behaviors often take over the living room to block out the painful feelings of the exiled parts when managers fail to keep them exiled.

ordinary distracter can't block it out, and so the distracter parts take on an extreme form. Schwartz calls them "firefighters" because they douse the fire of the pain by completely taking over the living room of consciousness.

Firefighters, although they are trying to help the system by keeping the pain away, create their own harmful results. Firefighter behaviors include anorexia and bulimia, substance abuse, extreme sexual behavior, and other self-destructive behavior, which can temporarily block out the psychological pain carried by the exiles. What all these behaviors have in common is that they completely fill the living room with sensory experience. This leaves no space for the painful feelings to flood the system. The problem with this strategy is that it is only temporary: eventually the stimulus conditions can't be sustained. When they are exhausted, a revived set of managers is likely to enter the living room. These are often harsh judges with recriminations about firefighter behavior, and firm resolutions not to let it happen again.

An Example of Firefighting: The Bulimic Loop

One of the more common Firefighter patterns is seen in bulimia. In fact it was working with a bulimic client that led Richard Schwartz to discover the IFS model over thirty years ago, as it provides a means to see a problematic behavior in its full systemic context. Bulimia is also a good illustration of how a part of the internal system that has a normal everyday function can be called into a more extreme role.

When an extreme inner critic takes over the living room, it can even distort how we see ourselves.

A person with bulimia usually has an inner system which has an extremely rigid inner critic part. This Critic is so strong that it takes up much of the living room and is constantly driving the person toward perfection.

As can be seen in this illustration, the critic/perfectionist part of this teenager is extreme. She has on her wall the goals for the week: eating almost nothing, running long distances and losing large amounts of weight. As she looks in the mirror she doesn't see herself accurately but through the eyes of an extreme inner Critic instead. This is a vivid example of how each part sees the world differently and how when parts are extreme they can dramatically distort the person's perceptions.

The binge eating of the bulimic is apt to begin when the person is feeling the crushing impossibility of ever meeting the Critic's standards.

The happy pig becomes extreme and now is a firefighter and takes over the living room to help block out the pain caused by the inner critic.

Feelings of unworthiness begin to flood into the living room and the alarm rings for the volunteer firefighters. In this case it is our Happy Pig who answers the call. While he is normally in charge of helping to get tasty food or sometimes takes on the role of distracter, in this emergency situation he is called into the role of firefighter. His job is to take over the whole living room to block out the bad feelings and he is ready to help.

Just as he is ready to dig in, the inner Critic says something about calories, but this time the rebel part steps up in coalition with the firefighter Happy Pig and says, "I don't give a damn about your ideas," pushes the Critic out of the living room so that Happy Pig is free to do his job.

Alas, even Happy Pig can only eat for so long.

The rebel part works to fend off the inner critic.

After the eating binge the inner critic takes over and the loop begins again.

When he stops, the Critic comes back into the living room, the bulimic vomits her food and now sits in despair with the Happy Pig, who also feels remorse. He thought he was helping but somehow it didn't work out.

The teenager goes to sleep. When she wakes up in the morning, the Critic is again in charge and she makes new goals for herself.

In order to change these self-destructive loops, it is necessary to understand all these parts and their interactions.

Healing through Parts Work

IFS therapy provides a focused and effective approach to this kind of repetitive cycle that people get trapped in. A person who has a high degree of internal polarization and exiled parts needs to work with an experienced IFS therapist. The following is an outline of how the therapeutic process might proceed with such an inner dynamic.

The first task is to spend time opening up space in the system for the Self. The therapist does this by working with the managers, in this case the critic part that is most involved in this cycle. The therapist would start by inviting the client to imagine their inner critic in their mind. The therapist would then ask the client to become aware of how she felt about it. It is likely in this case that a variety of parts of the client would react. For example a rebel part would probably pop up and talk about how tired she is of having the Critic drive the system so hard.

After listening to the rebel and acknowledging that it too was trying to help the system, the therapist would ask it to step back to watch the work with the Critic. Returning to the Critic, the therapist would again ask the client for her reactions to Critic. It could be that the Happy Pig would share how exhausted it is over the extra work load, which doesn't seem to be helping to keep the exiles at bay. The therapist would listen to that part, acknowledge it, and then ask it to step back to watch the work from a distance.

Returning to work with the Critic, the therapist asks how she sees the Critic now. Perhaps her image of the Critic is less severe and she is curious to understand this part better. At this point the therapist knows that the client's Self is available for the inner work, and can now get to know the Critic better by asking why it does what it does. What is it afraid would happen if it stopped? When did it start doing this for the person?

Now it is likely that the Critic will emerge as a part that is trying to protect a vulnerable child part that has been traumatized, and the child part will slowly emerge. The Critic will perhaps state that it is so strict with the client in order to keep her from being criticized and rejected, as she was in the past, which would further wound her child parts and flood the system with painful memories. Acknowledging the Critic's positive intention, the therapist would help it to see how the protective strategy is not actually working. Interestingly enough it is often the case with this type of protective manager part that it was not aware of the damaging effects it was having on the system. The therapist then asks the part, "If there were another way to keep that vulnerable part safe, would you be willing to shift your strategy?" The answer to this is usually yes, but with skepticism. It usually takes some time for such protector parts to learn to trust the Self.

Parts develop this trust by watching the inner work. So the next step is to ask the Critic to step back to watch the work. Once the client is in the Self, the therapist can carefully begin the work with the exile, in this case the young part carrying the unworthy feelings.

Exiled parts need to be carefully reintegrated into the system.

This illustration, taken from a client's experience with exiles, shows the lamp of Self being carried toward the exiles as the work begins. These exiles carry a variety of fears. It could be that they fear

they will be abandoned, as had happened in the past, if they don't meet the expectations of those they love. They may believe they have to hold on to memories of traumas they have experienced to keep it from happening again. A benefit of the parts work process is that the therapist doesn't have to figure this out. He or she has to support the inquiry process, helping the client to be in the Self and letting the client's Self guide the process. What heals the system and allows the Critic to shift out of its extreme role is to work with the exiles and to free them from the burdens which threaten the system. Being able to work with Self in the lead is what allows the process to take place. It takes a trained and experienced therapist to guide the process.

Therapeutic work with exiles can be very intense. The experienced therapist does not bring the exiles into the client's living room until the system has the resources to stay in the Self; otherwise the work will set off another critic/firefighter sequence. Sometimes therapists who use uncovering techniques without stabilizing the system with the Self make this mistake.

The skilled IFS therapist can help the client to encounter the exiles in the presence of the Self and thereby help the person hear the exiled parts' stories without being flooded by the pain. The therapist and the client's Self both witness the story and bring the necessary resources to the exiled parts. The loving encounter between the client's Self and the exiled parts is one of the most profound moments in the therapeutic process. This often happens with the sense of the exiled part being held in a loving embrace by the Self.

After the story of the exile is witnessed it often becomes clear that the exiled part is carrying some burdens. These could be beliefs, pain or wounds the exiled part is carrying. These burdens and beliefs can be released or transformed as a closing step in this sequence of the inner work.

Unburdening

One client, whom I will call Joan, discovered during therapy that a child part of her was burdened by the impact of her mother's constant practice of finding fault with her. As a child, she had always been forced to put away her own needs for recognition in order to meet the narcissistic needs of her mother or else face punishment.

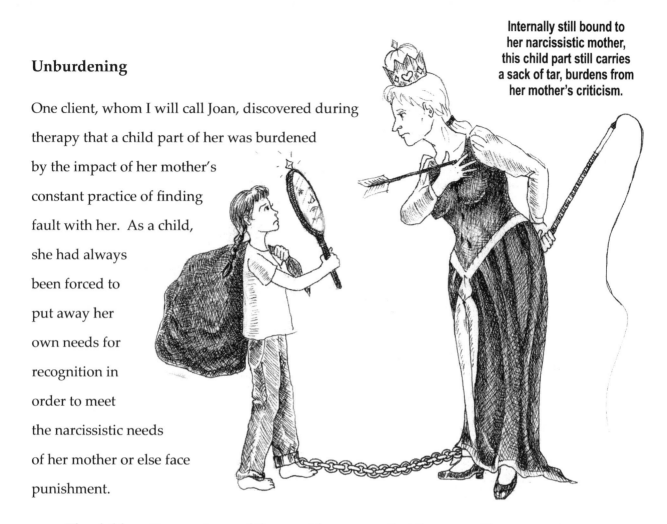

Internally still bound to her narcissistic mother, this child part still carries a sack of tar, burdens from her mother's criticism.

The child part's experience of these putdowns was that they were like a kind of tar that covered her. During the initial stages of the unburdening, the tar was gathered into a bag, but the little girl part still struggled to carry the burden.

In one session I asked her if she was ready to release these burdens. She had been unable to do so earlier because she feared losing her mother's love. She could not let them go until she had been released from the chain that bound her to her mother. She felt she still needed this connection to her mother. As Self came more into leadership and she was aware of all of the resources of her adult self, she now realized that she could be free from the chain binding her to this past experience of her mother's narcissism.

I asked her what she wanted to do with the tar. She said she wanted to mix it with gravel and make a path and she then imagined doing it. This was the beginning of the therapeutic journey for the client. There was much more work to do, more deeply buried exiles to recover; but she was able to free herself from the "tar" she had received in childhood and turn it into a path that led her toward healing.

After the therapeutic process has freed the client from the burdens, they are transformed into a path towards deeper healing.

Once the vulnerable part that carried these painful memories released its burdens, it could again become part of the system. The therapist helped it find its place with the other parts. When the return of an exile occurs, the therapist must also spend time helping the whole system adjust to this shift. It is the nature of living systems that whenever one part of the system changes the entire balance of the system changes. Therefore the whole system must be addressed as it adjusts to the return of the exiled part.

Working with firefighters and exiles is a central part of therapy with people who have experienced trauma. It takes special training and experience in IFS therapy to work effectively with these powerful dynamics.

However, in many cases we can recognize everyday distracters in our lives and can benefit from determining whether or not these distracter parts offer the most useful strategies for our system. Of course, it is not a problem to watch TV at the end of a long work day, or eat or drink to feed our Happy Pig. But some activities leave us truly refreshed and energized while others don't. These days, with an abundance of consumer products and amusements at our fingertips we may find ourselves automatically distracting. While this may seem to give us a break, it may not be giving our system the renewal it needs. The following exercise is designed to help you explore how to shift from automatic and less helpful distractions to activities that are genuinely restorative.

Distracter Awareness

1. Think about your typical day. At what points do you find yourself going to an automatic distracter? Radio on in the morning? Reading the newspaper while eating?

2. Look at transition times, empty spaces. What do you fill them with?

3. List your most common distracters. What seems to be their function? How do you feel afterwards? Are they working for you?

4. Reflect on the habitual thought patterns that precede the distracters. Jot down the messages in these thoughts. Store these messages in a spot where you can tend to them at a later time, reassuring the parts that are sending them.

5. Now think about what truly relaxes you. What allows you to let go of the tensions of the day and feel refreshed?

6. Can you imagine substituting one of these relaxing moments for one of the less effective distracting activities? Try experimenting and simply notice the effects. Let those guide you.

Chapter 8

Connecting to Inner Guidance
"Window to your soul"

Early in the development of IFS, Richard Schwartz began to find parts that seemed to be essentially different from those he had previously discovered. He called these guide parts, because they offered wisdom and guidance to the client's inner system.

My first encounter with guide parts came nearly twenty years ago in the first few years I was offering IFS therapy. During a session, a client I will call Martha, experienced an image of light from which emerged an exiled child part. It seemed that this light had protected the child part for many years until her system was ready and conditions were safe enough to receive it. It was a significant milestone to have this child part find its place in Martha's system, and we took the necessary time to help the other parts adjust to this new arrival. I was struck by the fact that in her psyche she had a mechanism to protect her vulnerable parts by sheltering them in light.

As we finished this stage of the work the light returned. At the time I was working with Nancy, a co-therapist I was training in the IFS model, and she encouraged Martha to ask the light what it was. Martha was quiet for a while, and then softly said, "Window . . . window to your soul." Later she said that it was as if she was looking into the face of God. It took some time for her to speak as, deeply moved, she sat in blissful tears.

Nancy and I marveled at what we were witnessing. I had been interested in the integration of spirituality and psychotherapy for many years, but was struggling to find the best way to do this. So imagine my amazement when a client suddenly had a spontaneous epiphany in my office - in a secular community mental health center!

Working with clients, I had always kept spirituality and psychotherapy separate out of a sense of professionalism. I told myself that if people came to a mental health clinic they were looking for secularly-oriented services; otherwise they would have gone to a religiously based counseling institution. At the same time, however, I felt that I was overlooking a powerful internal resource by not engaging the client's spiritual life. What was remarkable about Martha's experience was that it didn't result from any intentional integration of spirituality and psychotherapy on my part, but instead was something that arose naturally from the client's own inner work.

It has been my experience that spiritual resources are often available and are an important part of inner work. These spiritual resources, or guides, may appear in many forms and they are usually experienced as an interactive living presence. They may take the form of a nonspecific abstract presence, a light, or more specifically appear as a sage or religious figure like Jesus or Sophia. The quality of these guides is always wise and loving. Interestingly, while they are often available, they usually wait to be invited into the work.

Window to your Soul

What follows is a transcript from the ending of this session I have just described. I am working with my co-therapist Nancy and our client, Martha. Earlier in the session Martha had imagined placing her other parts in a room. The image of a light appeared, out of which a small child emerged. In the process of working with this child part, Martha experienced a repressed memory of a disturbing trauma that she had witnessed when she was a child.

I asked Martha to find out what the child part needed and how that could be provided. This process progressed smoothly and the child part felt comforted.

Then Martha reported a transparent form moving back and forth across her chest. She said it was the same light from which the child had emerged. My co-therapist, Nancy asked if this part had a name. The following sequence occurred:

Martha: "Yes . . . Window . . . Window to your soul . . . . I don't see anything but the light."

Nancy: "Does the light have a voice?"

Martha: "Yes, it says, 'It's time you asked.'" [Inwardly, Martha asked the voice if there was something more she needed to do for the traumatized child. She then reported back.]. "The information it gave me is that we looked at that, and there is a truth in that, but not to get tied up in that [traumatic event] . . . It is not necessary to go back into it again. I double checked that, because I don't want to cop out . . . Yes, it says, 'You can go back if you want, but it won't get you anywhere other than where you are now . . . What is is what is.' The phrase, 'Trust yourself'. . . . It is time to move on. Then it said, 'You are a power unto yourself . . . no need to be afraid.'"

Often the inner work can be a window to one's spiritual life.

[Long silence ...voice filled with emotion]

"It's a . . . It is almost like looking up and seeing God . . . It is just rushing down . . . Kind of piped or coming right down into me."

Nancy: "How does it feel?"

Martha: "It is very moving . . . I can't believe it is happening . . . it touched me . . . This is the God in us?"

[A prolonged silence]

Tom: "From that place with those feelings . . . can you visit the other parts?" [her other parts that are waiting in the room]

Martha: "When I brought that focus back to them . . . They were all talking quietly. When I came into the room, they fell silent. It was like they were in awe . . . the word 'power' comes to mind. But they were not fearful . . . A voice says, . . . 'She knows the truth.'"

[crying]

"A voice from somewhere . . . it must be the voice of God? It is saying, . . . 'All the answers are within me . . . and I am truly a magnificent creature.'"

[Pause, filled with emotion]

"I am feeling a lot of love and peace . . . And the voice keeps saying, . . . 'It is okay. Just keep feeling that . . . I'm just feeling a little overwhelmed now . . . The word trust keeps coming . . . and the loving . . . It's just, . . . 'Stay in the loving . . . in the lovingness . . . feel that and live your life from that.' That's all I figured out. . . . That is the answer and key to everything."

[A long pause]

Tom: "Anything any part wants to say at this point?"

Martha: "The Compassionate Self just said, 'Thank you.' Reached up and touched me on the forehead . . . and said, 'Thank you . . .' There was a real peace and lovingness."

Since this session I have often seen many clients who experience similar encounters during therapy. These are some of the most moving and meaningful experiences of my life. In such moments it feels as if one is in touch with a vast loving presence that is always there but has been forgotten. Somehow, at certain moments in the therapeutic process this deep, compassionate and loving presence becomes immediate and real. Thus an important focus of my work now is to better understand how I can best train other therapists to awaken and invite this presence into the therapeutic process.

An important question to consider is what the nature of the impact of this spiritual encounter is on the client's everyday life. Is it a type of peak experience separate from everyday life, or does it shift the person's internal system in some significant way? The progress that Martha made after encountering this kind of guidance is similar to what I have observed in others: there is no ongoing "nirvana:" all problems do not dissolve. But after this type of experience there is an ever-increasing access to Self, and the person makes an accelerated progress in both inner and outer work. Martha made considerable gains in her personal integration during subsequent sessions. She gradually moved out of a destructive relationship which she had been in for years and began to form new and more balanced relationships.

In every person there are inner healing resources. Parts work therapy can help us to access them.

The great gift of Martha's work was to show me in a clear and dramatic way that internal resources of healing power can be found within all of us. Helping people to access them is an important aspect of the therapy that I offer.

The Nature of Spiritual Experiences

One of the first things I did after the session with Martha was to see if there was a way to tap this kind of experience in my own inner therapeutic work. I have always believed that it is a good idea to receive therapy using the model one is learning in order to know it from the inside out. In my own inner work, I too had an experience of encountering a source of guidance, though it was not as powerful, dramatic or clear as Martha's; in some ways it was more typical. I experienced a connection to something that appeared as a light. I had a wonderful and peaceful feeling while connected with the image. I asked this image if it had any guidance for me and it replied that all I needed to do was breathe with awareness and it would be present with me. It was not a dramatic epiphany, but it turned out to be wonderful and profound advice. Encounters with a source of guidance may be more or less dramatic, but they usually are quite profound. One thing is certain. Each person's experience is unique, so it is important not to have expectations about how inner guidance will unfold.

Since these early events, I began to actively invite my clients to explore their spiritual lives. Aside from increasing the pace and the effectiveness of the therapy itself, the spiritual connections which clients make in therapy positively affect their overall spiritual life, bringing a renewed vitality and deeper personal meaning into their everyday lives.

Healing Presence

Another client, whom I will call Cheryl, was a member of a fairly conservative Christian church. To assist in the process of therapy I had invited her to seek inner spiritual guidance, since I knew this was an important aspect of her life. She very readily reported an image of Jesus and felt great comfort in his presence. In the course of therapy I would often ask her to call on Jesus if she was feeling overwhelmed or in need of guidance.

One of Cheryl's painful psychological conflicts was rooted in the fact that she had had an abortion when she was younger. When she encountered her memory of the abortion in our imagery work she became overwhelmed by guilt-ridden and judging parts, and the Self was not available. I remember the internal conflict I had at this time: I was questioning the wisdom of asking her to seek Jesus' assistance when she felt so much condemnation coming from the church. However, the quality of the presence she had always reported when Jesus appeared was so full of loving compassion and wisdom that I decided that this was the right course. I suggested that she could invite Jesus to help her. She wanted to do this.

The nature or form of the inner guidance is unique for each person.

Cheryl reported having an image of Jesus soothing her young woman part, who carried the experience of the abortion. This young woman part was in anguish about what she had done. Cheryl reported Jesus showing her an image of the child in his embrace and reassuring her that it was with him. He then took the young woman part to a place of healing where she could recover from the trauma she had experienced. There remained work to do regarding her guilt about the abortion, but the tormented quality of the obsessions subsided, and the presence of Jesus was available to aid in the rest of the work.

Transfer of Self Energy

In a later session Cheryl interrupted the work we were doing and said that Jesus had requested her attention. In my experience this is not so common; usually these inner guides wait to be invited in. In this instance Jesus wanted to offer her communion. She reported that he said, "This is my body; take, eat in remembrance of me," and did the same with his blood. It was a deeply moving experience, remarkable in its impact. Prior to this experience Cheryl found it difficult to experience the qualities of Self without having the image of Jesus present. After this session, she seemed to have absorbed Self qualities into her own system, and they became more present in her everyday life.

From this I gained a new understanding of how one might view the communion experience. Perhaps spiritual figures represent concentrated Self energy. Communion could be seen as a process whereby this energy is transferred from a greater Self, perhaps a Divine Self, to our personal Self.

Some Cautions about Guides

Other insights about guides came from the inner work of a therapist I will call Sue, who took part in IFS therapy as part of her training. When asked if she had an inner source of spiritual guidance she did not report a religious figure but rather a globe of light that transformed the atmosphere of her surroundings in a peaceful way. Her subsequent experience with this globe of light reveals some of the risks inherent in working with this kind of internal force.

She had been working with a part that she called the Performer. The Performer was remarkably skilled in pulling off a balancing act on the high wire, riskily juggling all the demands of professional life. Many of

Sue's other parts, however, were becoming exhausted through the effort and anxiety required to sustain this act. Through an inner dialogue the Performer agreed to come down off the high wire, but this part then went into a depression. In an effort to help it adjust and find a new and more balanced role, Sue brought the globe of light over to be with the Performer. This had an amazingly transforming effect. The Performer was not only renewed, it actually became an almost superhuman force. This caused a backlash of fear with Sue's other parts. I was concerned about this fear and certainly curious how this would play out, but it was near the end of the session, so I had to leave the work at this point.

This "performer part" thought it could do everything at once with the greatest of ease, but it was causing great stress to the person's inner system.

When she came in the next week Sue reported being very energized, but also noted some problematic relationship issues that needed to be addressed. In the process of this work we began to identify an angry part that was seen as a bear in a cage. As we began a dialogue with the caged bear the whole image suddenly vanished. When parts disappear it is usually because other parts are blocking them out or stopping the process. It is standard procedure to have the client check to see whether there are any parts that are stopping the imagery work. Sue did the internal check and the Performer part came forward in all her glory and said that she had stopped the imagery because there was no need to deal with petty feelings like anger - she was "beyond all that!"

Then a whole group of Sue's parts started complaining about how the Performer had been pushing them around and not giving them any space all week long. Sue decided to have a conference with these disgruntled parts and as a result decided to separate the globe of light from the Performer. As Sue did this the system came back into balance. Additional work was needed, however, so that the Performer could come to terms with her diminished role.

This experience illustrates that it is usually unhealthy for ambitious or perfectionist parts receiving an infusion of "spiritual" energy. Perhaps this explains why some charismatic spiritual leaders, be they Christian, Hindu or Islamic, sometimes become so imbalanced in their everyday lives, developing extravagant or exploitive life styles at odds with the messages they preach. When spiritual energy attaches to a striving, critical or perfectionist part, great imbalances can arise in the system, as the person attempts to transcend his or her humanity and take on godlike qualities. My experience is that when genuine spiritual qualities enter through the Self, the person can accept and embrace all of his or her parts and a harmonious cooperation takes place. Through this process the system can experience both transcendence as well as balance in everyday life.

When "Guides" Are Not Guides

There is another important lesson from Sue's work with the inner globe of light. At one point the globe of light appeared, but it was demanding and bossy. This is not the normal behavior of authentic guide parts. They usually have no agenda for the person other than affirming and assisting

What may first appear as a spiritual guide can turn out to be something quite different.

in some way. Because of this discrepancy, I was suspicious and decided to check out this globe of light, "guide part." I suggested to Sue that she ask this part what it was, and when she did an impish part suddenly jumped out of the light. It said that it had disguised itself as the light because it felt that was the only way it could get her attention. This illustrates the potential imbalance that could come from valuing only the "higher" spiritual aspects of the inner world – all parts have value, – and parts are not always what they appear to be.

The protector parts often need a lot of recognition and reassurance before they can step back.

The Transforming Power of Guides

The capacity for spiritual guides to transform extreme parts is illustrated in the work of a client I will call Joan. Earlier, Joan had worked with a part she called Warrior that had been relentlessly driving her even though she needed to rest and heal from an illness. I asked the Warrior what she feared would happen if she stopped driving Joan. She said she feared Joan would die. The Warrior believed that she had actually been keeping Joan alive. Indeed, this part had been very important in helping Joan to survive many life-threatening health crises, and Warrior wanted me to fully understand this.

It was important for the Warrior to be acknowledged for what she offered, and as we did this, she relaxed, – somewhat. Still, the Warrior wanted to block efforts to dialogue with a part she called the Invalid and wanted to keep this part in exile. The Warrior was unwilling to relinquish the living room; she was convinced that the survival of the system depended upon her staying in control. This is often the case with protector parts that have had to work hard and carry heavy loads.

At the beginning of the session I had talked with Joan about her inner spiritual resources, and she described a spiritual guide whom she referred to as Sophia. Given that the Warrior was unwilling to step back and leave space for Self, I suggested that Joan gather her parts in a healing place of safety and invite spiritual assistance into this sacred space. Sophia appeared and instructed Joan's parts to form a circle. Sophia reassured the parts that they would not be flooded with overwhelming emotion and that it was to the benefit of the system to have this discussion. Sophia's presence softened the Warrior's harsh stance. Finally she allowed the Invalid to speak. The

Inner guides can assist the system in accepting the exiles safely back into the system.

Invalid had a lot to say about her suffering. Sophia spent considerable time enlightening the Warrior and the other parts on the importance of accepting and caring for this part; it was Joan's physical body, and Joan depended upon her body for her existence! .The Warrior understood, but when Sophia asked all of the parts to welcome the Invalid part into the circle

and to hold hands, the Warrior refused to hold Invalid's hand. Sophia just smiled and then asked, "Who will hold her hands?" Joan's Nurturing part and her Nature Girl part came forward. Taking the hands of the Invalid, they brought her into the circle.

In the weeks following this session the effects of the Invalid's presence on the other parts became a major theme. It took some time for her system to rebalance. When Joan began to give time for her body to rest and no longer drove herself to overwork, her Critic part began to berate her for being lazy and worthless. When Joan came into the next therapy session the rest of her system was totally fed up with the Critic and wanted it banned from the system.

A Monk part that Joan had found in an earlier session suggested that they all go on an inner vision quest. The parts seemed excited about this but thought that the Critic Part should be excluded. My experience of the inner system shows that it is counter-productive to ban a part. Every effort should be made to find a way to understand what the unpopular part is trying to do for the system so that it can find its natural place. I managed to convince the other parts that it was worth trying to understand the Critic before going on the vision quest. In exploring what the Critic was doing for the system it became clear that she was trying to protect Joan from outside criticism, the harshness of which had been devastating to her when she was young. The Critic believed that if Joan was perfect she wouldn't be criticized and hurt by people on the outside. She wanted Joan to be perfect; it was for her own good!

It is often the case that the return of an exiled part is not welcome by some parts.

I asked the Critic if there were a way to keep Joan from being hurt other than constant criticism. Would she consider easing off? The Critic agreed to consider that possibility, and reported that she was exhausted by having to carry this load for so many years. She said she would be relieved if there was another way. However, she deeply feared that this meant she was no longer needed. This is a common fear of parts, especially managers and protectors who have been carrying heavy loads. I reassured the Critic that there would always be something for her to do; it might just take another form. The Critic softened considerably.

The inner critic and the little Baptist girl have absorbed word for word the expectations of the critical parent and the church.

At this point another part emerged, which Joan called the Little Baptist Girl. This part seemed to be attached to the Critic, and it had definite ideas about what was right and wrong with Joan. The Little Baptist Girl came into existence because one of the sources of hurtful external criticism had come from a very conservative Baptist community. The Critic and the Little Baptist Girl were a powerful coalition, which had plagued Joan with their constant berating since she was young. I asked the other parts if they were willing to have these two parts come along on the vision quest and they agreed, although not without reservations.

This inner vision quest was remarkable in several ways. Not surprisingly, Joan found Sophia on the journey; but in addition, Jesus appeared. This was a great surprise to Joan since she had long ago left behind her Christian beliefs because of the humiliating pain she had experienced from the church as she was growing up.

It turned out that it was important for the Critic and the Little Baptist Girl to have come along on this vision quest, because they were the focus of the work. It is very often the case that the parts of us we want to exclude have vitally important qualities for the system once they are released from their extreme forms. On the vision quest Sophia approached the Critic part, laid her hands on the Critic's weak, fault-finding eyes and restored her vision to wholeness. Sophia announced that the Critic would now be called Integrity and that her new job in the system was to direct Joan with Self-imbued personal integrity instead of externally imposed "shoulds and oughts." The ruler, which the Critic used to measure and evaluate everything she did in the past, was replaced with a compass pointing toward her heart. In the months to come, Integrity would play an important role in providing guidance in the course of Joan's daily life.

Sophia assists the "inner critic" in transforming into her true function, "Integrity".

The client was surprised to find that an inner guide in the form of Jesus freed her Baptist girl from her black- and- white thinking.

Then, Jesus approached the Little Baptist Girl and healed her narrow black-and-white vision. He announced that her new name would be Faith, and he replaced the Bible that she tightly held with the radiant light of the living word centered in her heart. Faith offered Joan a sense of trust in her own inner spiritual truth which had previously been discouraged by the church.

As often happens after this kind of inner work the session closed with the parts coming into a circle, with the guide part in the middle and the circle symbolizing a return to Self.

All of the parts can be included when we find Self, sometimes with the help of an inner guide.

Discussion and Conclusions

Frankly, I don't know how to understand these experiences from a scientific, objective perspective. It is very clear, however, that these people have had an authentic experience of inner guidance that offers profound resources for their healing. Somehow they are able find an inner connection to a deep and compassionate state from which they are able to find both guidance and wisdom.

I am deeply moved by witnessing the loving presence that people encounter in the course of this process. I find my own life is tremendously enriched by the experiences of my clients. I also experience a deep sense of peace that comes from those moments graced with deep spiritual connections. Furthermore, I find that when I am able to work from Self, I am renewed by participating in the therapeutic process rather than finding myself relying on my manager parts who work so hard and lead me to burn-out.

In light of these discoveries, it seems that one of our most important roles as therapists is to assist clients in connecting to their spiritual sources of healing and wisdom. Many people experience this wisdom and guidance as coming from a source within themselves. For others, it seems to come from a connection to sources of spiritual guidance outside themselves.

If a person is able to find this kind of guidance, it has been my experience that the therapeutic process moves much faster, especially in cases where there was trauma in their earlier life experience. As I have noted, my understanding of the reason for this is that these sources of guidance have concentrated Self qualities. When guides enter the system they lend these Self qualities to the process. This means that when a person uncovers a part that is carrying the memory and pain of a traumatic experience, that part can be helped from a place of calm, compassionate wisdom.

Without such a spiritual resource the therapist must proceed slowly to bring Self into a leadership role before the system is ready to deal with the traumatized part. If the therapist fails to do this these traumatized exiles will threaten to flood the system with the pain of the memory, the firefighters will act out and the rigid managers will come back in force. In the traumatized system the reestablishment of the Self can take a long time, but if spiritual guidance is available the healing is accelerated, extreme parts are more readily transformed and exiled parts more easily comforted and safely brought back into the system. The presence of a guide allows Self leadership to develop much faster as well. It is a humbling and freeing experience for the therapist. If genuine guides are there to offer a powerful source of healing, then the main job of the therapist is to help the client access that source.

It can be beneficial for the therapist to explore a client's spiritual experiences early in the therapy process, and to listen for cues that may indicate the presence of a guide. However, the therapist should be careful not to impose such an idea on the client. The guided imagery exercise found at the end of this chapter may be useful to help clarify sources of guidance that might be available for inner work. At the same time it is important for the therapist not to become enamored with the idea that this spiritual source is available to fix everything. In all instances the most important work is accessing the Self, understanding the parts, and working to bring balance to the system. The therapist can offer the option of inviting in a source of guidance if it seems that it might be useful. He or she must rely on the client's judgment about whether to do this or not.

What does this mean for the practitioner? It appears to me that the spiritual connections that emerge in parts work have an undeniable ability to transform the internal systems of clients. These spiritual guides appear to be fundamental forces moving the system toward balance and equilibrium. They possess a deep wisdom and knowledge about the client and offer a peaceful and loving state of mind. This is an invaluable aid when the clients confront pain and trauma in their system. Perhaps most important, because these resources arise out of the client's own experience, they support the client's own sense of wholeness. They are always available if one can remember to access them.

The following exercise is a guided imagery experience that can help connect with sources of inner guidance. I use it in workshops and with clients so that we all can have this inner resource to draw on during our inner work.

Finding Your Inner Guide

Please use the following directions to help design a guided imagery, adjusting, deleting or adding elements to make them fit your sense of what will work best for you. You can create a tape that you can play for yourself, or have someone read it to you. It also works well to do this as a group exercise. It is important that you know that you are in charge of your experience. Use what feels appropriate for you. While reading this guided imagery it is important to set a pace that gives space for the imagery to unfold. I have placed . . . at points where you might want to pause.

Beginning Directions

This is a journey to a place of healing, a place where you might encounter a source of spiritual guidance. We will first spend some time relaxing, letting go of tension, and coming to our center.

- Become aware of your breathing.
- "Breathing in, I am aware of breathing in." (On the in-breath think "in.")
- "Breathing out, I am aware of breathing out." (On the out-breath think "out. . . ")
- "Breathing in, I calm my body and mind." (On the in-breath think "calm.")
- "Breathing out, I release tensions." (On the out-breath think "release. . . . ")
- Be aware with each breath your body can become more relaxed, more calm. . . . .
- Scan your body for any remaining tension. Breathe ease and calm into those areas as you release the tension.

Finding a Peaceful Place

- Imagine yourself on the edge of a beautiful area in nature . . . You notice a path that you sense will lead you to a peaceful healing place, a place where you can feel safe, find rest and guidance . . .
- When you are ready begin along the path . . . feel your feet connecting with the ground. Smell the scent of the air . . . the sounds of nature . . .
- Be aware of any landscape you pass along the way . . . You may travel along a valley or up a hill. It is possible that there will be water in your landscape . . . Move along the path that will lead you to this place of peace and calm . . .
- Gradually, find your self approaching a beautiful, peaceful, safe, place . . .
- When you have arrived at your place of peace and healing, spend some time exploring it and breathing in its atmosphere. . . . What are the surroundings like?

Are there trees or other plant life? . . . Is there water -- a pool, waterfall or lake? Allow the peaceful qualities of this place to penetrate deep into your being. . . .

Receiving Guidance

- You may notice somewhere a special place that seems made just for you where you can sit and relax even more deeply. . . . If you like you might approach this place and sit or lie down. . . . You feel comfortable but alert knowing that here is a place where you can invite your source of guidance to be present. . . .

- You gradually become aware of a source of guidance; you sense a wise and loving presence. . . . The guidance could appear in many ways; simply as a feeling that you have, as a figure, a voice, or a light. Whatever the form, you should feel safe, cared for and loved in its presence. . . .

- Allow your sense of this presence to clarify. . . . You have a feeling of being deeply understood and cared for.. . . . Become aware of how you can communicate with this source of guidance. . . . Make contact with it. . . . Perhaps it has a name? . . . Let the source know you would like its guidance. . . . Perhaps you have a question?. . . . Do whatever you need to do in this place of peace and healing. . . .

Bringing the session to a close

- Take some time to finish your sharing with your source of guidance. . . . You might ask how you can bring its presence into your everyday life. . . . How can you carry back what you have experienced? . . .

- You may receive a symbol that will help you remember your experience. . . . something to remind you that you can return to this place at any time. . . .

- Now begin to prepare to depart from this place of peace and healing. . . . You may want to thank your source of guidance. . . . When you are ready, begin to go back along the path back to your everyday consciousness. It may be the same path or a different path. . . . Take your time returning. . . . You are aware that soon you will return to your everyday consciousness feeling refreshed and alert, bringing with you the memory of this inner journey.

- As you arrive back gently bring your attention to your breath. . . . being aware of breathing in while breathing in, out while breathing out. . . . Bring your awareness to your body, feeling the peacefulness you carry with you flow through your body.

- Begin to move your fingers and hands. . . . stretch and bring your attention back to the room. . . . And when you are ready, open your eyes . . . return to everyday consciousness refreshed and alert.

Afterword

We created this book with the intention of giving you some ways of understanding yourself and others through this parts work model. We have shared our insights into how and why our inner system works the way it does. Some readers will find that through this book they have already begun a journey of deeper understanding of themselves and others. Others will find that they are curious to experience this type of inner work themselves.

The last two chapters describe a process that has happened in intense therapy with therapists and clients who have considerable experience with this approach. Many people have reported finding healing just from reading this book. However, it can be beneficial to have a trained IFS therapist as a guide. This is particularly true when dealing with strong inner polarizations between parts or when there are traumatized parts. The IFS Institute has a listing of trained therapists at: https://ifs-institute.com/practitioners.

If you are already in therapy you might share with your therapist what you have found useful in this book and explore how you might use it in your work with them. If you are not in therapy but find yourself in crisis, we recommend that you seek help from resources such as a crisis center, community mental health center, or the religious counseling organization of your choice.

At the end of this chapter you will find a listing of IFS resources. The website developed by Richard Schwartz includes a list of therapists trained in the IFS model and suggestions of other readings about this inner work.

We welcome comments from you about the book: how it has been useful, how it could be improved. It is "a work in progress," and we intend to incorporate the feedback we get from readers and participants in workshops to improve future editions.

We wish you the very best as you continue your inner journey.

Tom, Lauri and Sharon

Parts Work /IFS Resources

www.wingedheart.org

- This is my website. There you will find more articles I have written, videos I have made, links to spiritual resources, as well as information on workshops I offer.

https://ifs-institute.com

- This is the IFS website for Richard Schwartz. If you click on the "resource" tab will see many resources including a "practitioner directory" that gives you a listing of IFS-trained therapists in your area.

Other books that offer you more in-depth reading about IFS are:

- Schwartz, Richard. (2001). *Introduction to the Internal Family Systems Model*. Oak Park, Il: The Center for Self Leadership. (For a general audience.)

- Schwartz, Richard. (1995). *Internal Family Systems Therapy*. New York: Guilford Press. (For therapists)

- Earley, Jay. (2009) *Self-Therapy: A Step-By-Step Guide to Creating Inner Wholeness Using IFS, A New, Cutting-Edge Therapy*. Mill City Press, Inc.

- Barbera, Mona (2008). *Bring Yourself to Love: How Couples Can Turn Disconnection into Intimacy and Creative Communication for a Naturally Spiritual Marriage/Committed Relationship, Using Internal Family Systems*. Dos Monos Press.

References

Introduction

Rowan, John (1990). *Subpersonalities: The People Inside Us.* New York: Routledge.

Thich Nhat Hanh (2001). *Transformation at the Base.* Berkeley, CA: Parallax Press.

Thich Nhat Hanh (2006) *The Nature of Mind.* Berkeley, CA: Parallax Press.

Schwartz, Richard. (2001). *Introduction to the Internal Family Systems Model.* Oak Park, Il: The Center for Self Leadership.

Schwartz, Richard. (1995). *Internal Family Systems Therapy.* New York: Guilford Press.

Chapter 1

Thich Nhat Hanh (2006) *The Nature of Mind.* Berkeley, CA: Parallax Press.

Thich Nhat Hanh (1989). Lectures on the Nature of Consciousness. Omega Institute, Rhinebeck, NY. Unpublished.

Chapter 2

Barks, Coleman & Green, Michael (1997). *The Illuminated Rumi.* New York: Broadway Books, 77.

Barks, Coleman (1987). *We are Three: New Rumi Poems* Athens, GA: Maypop Books, 44.

Brown, Molly (1983). *The Unfolding Self: Psychosynthesis and Counseling.* Los Angeles: Psychosynthesis Press, 11-12.

Frost, Robert (1943). *A Witness Tree.* London: J. Cape, 46.

Kunitz, Stanley (1995). *Passing Through: The Later Poems.* New York: W.W. Norton, 107.

Mitchell, Stephen, ed., (1993). *The Enlightened Heart: An Anthology of Sacred Poetry.* New York: Harper Perennial.

Schwartz, Richard. *The Internal Family Systems Model.* Center for Self Leadership, 2003. Accessed Jan. 9, 2022 https://ifs-institute.com/resources/articles/internal-family-systems-model-outline

Singer, June (1973). *Boundaries of the Soul: The Practice of Jung's Psychology.* Garden City, NY: Anchor Books. 271-272.

Whitman, Walt (1897). *Leaves of Grass.* Small, Maynard & Company. Original Harvard University, Digitized Sept. 27, 2005, on Google Books.

Chapter 6

Tolstoy, Leo. *Anna Karenina.* Trans. Richard Pevear and Larissa Volokhonsky (2002). New York: Penguin Classics, 704-706.

The Authors

Tom Holmes, PhD, is Professor Emeritus at Western Michigan University (WMU). He has been training graduate students in psychotherapy since 1985. From 1996 to 2006 he taught in the Holistic Health Care Program at WMU. His specialty area is spirituality and the therapeutic process. Tom received training in Internal Family Systems Therapy from Richard Schwartz in the late 1980's and has been teaching, training and practicing IFS since that time.

In recent years his focus has been on burnout prevention: "Healing the Healer" and "Tuning the Heart of the Healer." His workshops integrate Western psychology with Buddhist psychology and the Sufi path of the heart as well as spiritual teachings from Christianity, Judaism, and Taoism. He specializes in integrating spirituality with Parts Work.

Lauri Holmes, MSW, was Director of the Family Counseling Program at Family and Children Services of the Kalamazoo Area for twenty-two years where she did therapy, supervised therapists and did program development. Trained as a family therapist with Salvador Minuchin, she met Dick Schwartz in the late 80's at the Family Therapy Network Conference, and subsequently trained her staff in the "Parts Work" model. Since retiring she has assisted Tom in writing and workshop presentations as well pursuing a variety of interests in art, music and community service.

The Illustrator

Sharon Eckstein has a Master of Fine Art degree in painting and has taught art in public schools, at Western Michigan University and at the Kalamazoo Institute of Arts. She was a gallery artist for many years and has won numerous awards for her paintings. She also has a Masters degree in Counseling Psychology and incorporates art therapy into her private practice. She has been studying Internal Family Systems Therapy for several years.

Made in the USA
Las Vegas, NV
24 September 2023

77988774R00077